CW01506699

QUEERSTORY

LGBTQ+

In common use since the 1990s, LGBTQ+ is the root of an ever-evolving acronym that aims to encompass and embrace the wide spectrum of non-heterosexual and non-cisgender people in the world, and the movements that have organised to fight for their rights.

In order to avoid confusion, the acronym has been used as an umbrella term throughout this book. This may mean that LGBTQ+ sometimes retrospectively includes groups that would not have used the term to describe themselves. The word 'queer' has been used as an inclusive term to describe a varied and extensive history of LGBTQ+ communities and culture across the twentieth and twenty-first centuries.

ABOUT LINDA RILEY

A Stonewall award winner and Icon of the Year in 2018, Linda Riley has dedicated her career to promoting and protecting LGBTQ+ rights. She is a former director of US LGBTQ+ campaign group GLAAD and adviser to the British Labour Party on diversity issues. She is the current publisher of the iconic DIVA Magazine, Europe's leading magazine for LGBTQ+ women, as well as the founder of the Rainbow Honours and the European and British Diversity awards.

QUEERSTORY

An Infographic History of the Fight for LGBTQ+ Rights

Foreword by Linda Riley

CONTENTS

1 Before Stonewall

2 LGBTQ+ Liberation

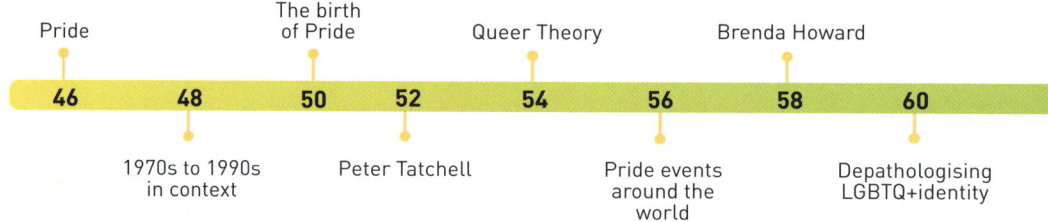
3 21st-Century Rights

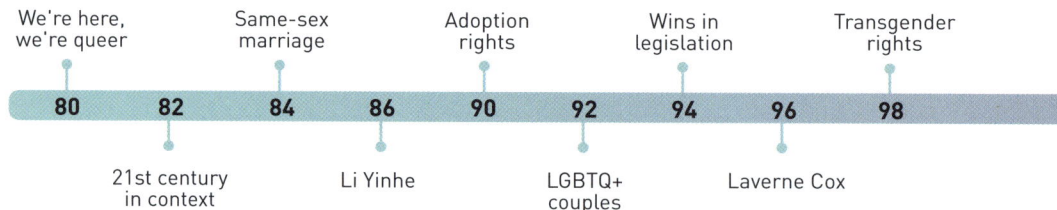

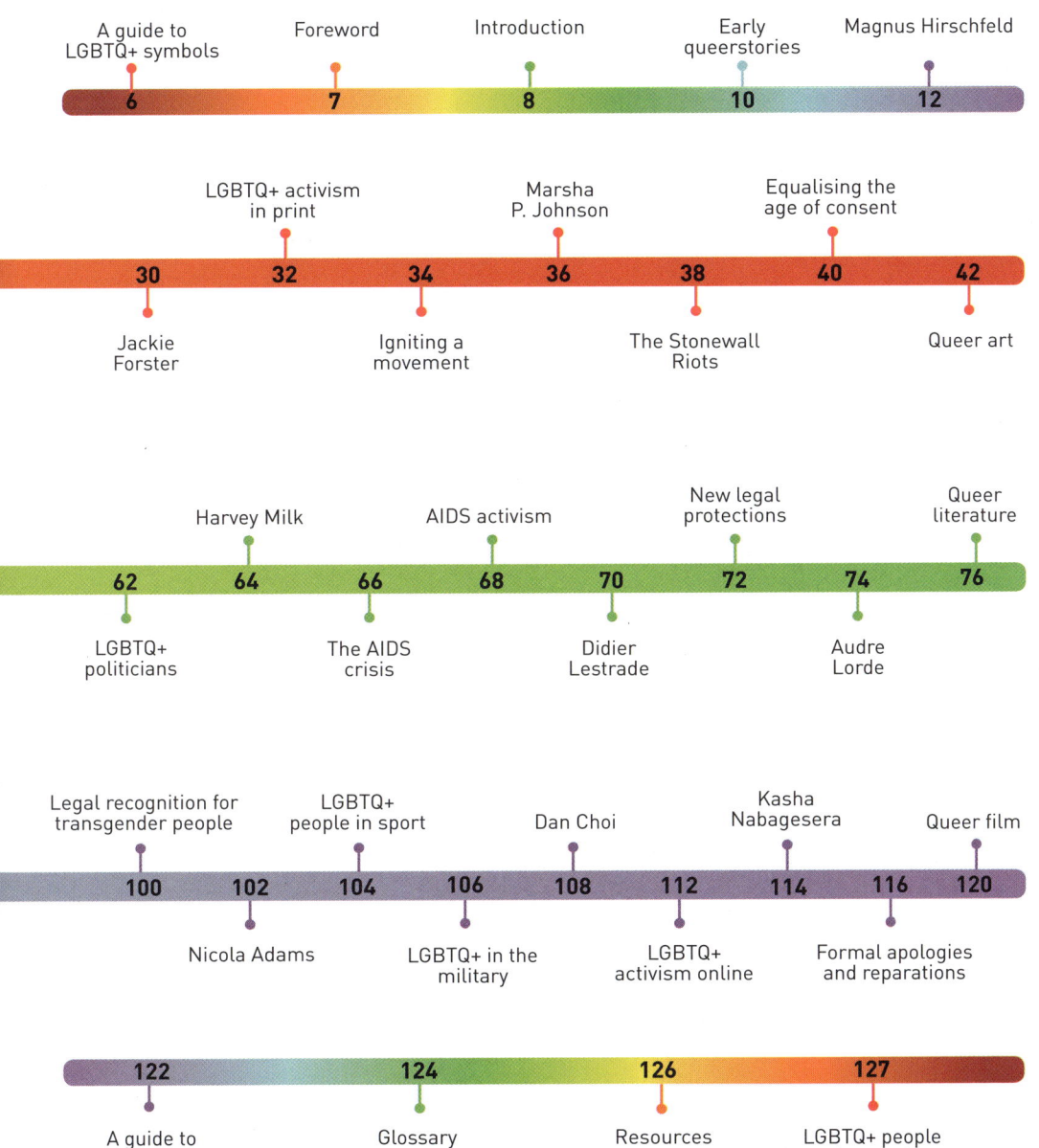

A guide to LGBTQ+ symbols

Throughout history, members of the LGBTQ+ community have used various symbols to express their identity. Some of these symbols, such as rings, handkerchiefs and flowers, originated as a secret way to indicate sexuality. Today, the LGBTQ+ symbols shown below are worn with pride.

MARS

Two interlocking Mars symbols, each symbolising the male gender, have been used to represent the gay community since the 1990s.

VENUS

Two interlocking Venus symbols, each of which symbolises the female gender, have often been used to represent the lesbian community.

TRANSGENDER

Trans activist Holly Boswell combined the Venus and Mars symbols in 1993. Her image is now used to represent the transgender community.

LAMBDA

The Greek letter L, or lambda, was originally associated with the Gay Liberation movement. In 1970, the Gay Activists Alliance in New York adopted it as its official symbol.

PANSEXUAL

The P-shaped symbol of pansexuality unites the male, female and transgender symbols into a new symbol.

PINK TRIANGLE

Originally used in Nazi concentration camps to single out gay men, the pink triangle was reclaimed as a symbol of pride by gay liberation activists in the 1970s.

DOUBLE MOON

Created by Vivian Wagner in 1998, the double moon is an alternative symbol to the pink triangle to represent bisexuality with less problematic associations.

LABRYS

A classical symbol originally representing female strength and independence, the labrys has been used to represent lesbian feminism since the 1970s.

Foreword by Linda Riley

QUEERSTORY: out and proud

At a time when LGBTQ+ rights have progressed beyond expectations, remembering the struggles faced to reach this point in our history feels vital. Understanding the expansive history behind our strong, wonderful and ever-evolving LGBTQ+ community takes precedence as the fight for LGBTQ+ rights is still ongoing in many parts of the world.

To encompass our entire queer story is an impossible task, but *Queerstory* showcases the integral elements: the activists, artists and scientists that made an extraordinary difference, paving the path that has moved us forward from the 1940s up until today.

We have reached a place where the future looks brighter than ever and the prospect of overcoming discrimination against LGBTQ+ people feels possible. However, that does not mean that the fight is over by any means – *Queerstory* should inspire us to keep campaigning and breaking down barriers.

Print has played a huge part in LGBTQ+ activism and as publisher of *DIVA* magazine, my work has played an integral role in bringing queer life into mainstream media, particularly members of the lesbian and bisexual community. This is a topic that I will always feel passionate about as an LGBTQ+ activist and I am proud that throughout my career I have seen unbelievable achievements.

Our liberation must be celebrated but the limitations that still remain must not be forgotten. I am filled with hope when I remember that LGBTQ+ marriages are now recognised and laws protect our community. I find comfort knowing there are strong communities and safe spaces for LGBTQ+ people all over the world.

Public acceptance of LGBTQ+ lives remains revolutionary, but we are powerful and determined to gain equality worldwide.

INTRODUCTION

It is difficult to pinpoint the moment at which the LGBTQ+ rights movement began. Long before we might imagine, there were remarkable pioneers like physician Magnus Hirschfeld, who spoke out against popular opinion to question society's mistreatment of queer people and educate the public on what it meant to be non-heterosexual, non-cisgender or non-conforming – often at a time when it was extremely dangerous to do so. However, until the mid-20th century, these were often solitary voices, making radical attempts to communicate their ideas within a climate of deep-rooted discrimination.

By the 1920s in Berlin there were clubs and newspapers for gay and lesbian people, and some LGBTQ+ individuals had begun to speak out against their oppression, organising demonstrations and rallies. In the 1930s in New York, the 'pansy craze' saw wild underground drag parties sweep the city, inviting a glorious gay subculture onto the main stages of Manhattan. A seed of pride and power was being sown in these discrete celebrations of LGBTQ+ identity across the globe, providing the catalyst for a call to arms across the queer community: to finally come together and demand respect, recognition and rights.

It was not until the 1940s, however, that LGBTQ+ activists began to effectively mobilise, gaining the strength to begin their formal fight for acceptance. This is where this book really begins, in the aftermath of World War II, at a time when societal norms were beginning to be questioned and the first LGBTQ+ rights organisations were springing up around the world. In the pages that follow, we are taken from the assembly of these 'homophile groups' all the way up to the present-day fight for trans rights and formal apologies to the LGBTQ+ community, via the Stonewall riots, the birth of Pride and activism after the AIDS crisis.

Key Each continent is represented by a different colour throughout the book

- Europe
- Asia
- North America
- South America
- Africa
- Oceania

In any brief history there is a necessary exclusion of many aspects of the story, and this is perhaps particularly true of an account of the fight for LGBTQ+ rights. Even the ever-expanding acronym of 'LGBTQ+' struggles to include all the varied groups and individuals it intends to, and the people under its umbrella make up a wide range of separate communities that are sometimes in profound disagreement with each other. This book offers only a selected overview of an overwhelmingly dense and complex movement, powered by countless inspiring individuals and groups who dedicated their lives to a better future for non-heterosexual and non-cisgender people.

Above all, the stories, timelines and biographies collected here serve as an illustration of the incredible resilience, bravery and optimism of the queer community in the face of discrimination, oppression and even catastrophe. Together, they are a testament to the great progress made so far and provide a jolt of empowerment to all of us facing the work still to be done.

EARLY QUEERSTORIES

Gender and sexuality have found expression in a variety of diverse ways throughout human history, with evidence existing in almost all ancient civilisations. Some historians suggest that it was not until the arrival of Christian and Islamic influences in the first millennium that queer people faced the kind of prejudices that LGBTQ+ communities are still trying to counter today.

c. 1000 BCE

As long ago as 1000 BCE, it is accepted in early Native American and First Nations cultures that the practice of multiple sex and gender roles and sexuality do not strictly define a person's gender. In 1990, the term **'two-spirit'** is created to encompass all the gender non-conforming terms used by traditional communities.

c. 600 BCE

Ancient Greek lyric poet **SAPPHO**, from the island of Lesbos, writes poems of love and sexual desire. She is praised by Plato and honoured in public statues. While many translators and scholars try to heterosexualise her poetry over the years, it is now accepted that her work celebrates love between women.

c. 400 BCE

An Indian text on the art of living, love and pleasure, the **KAMA SUTRA** is attributed to the ancient Indian philosopher Vātsyāyana. It includes various passages on homosexual relations (both between men and between women) and holds love and sexual fulfilment as one of the primary goals in life.

c. 385 BCE

PLATO's *Symposium* celebrates the practice of homosexual relationships, a standard social norm in ancient Greece. The *Symposium* especially praises the pedagogic benefits of these relationships for adolescents. It is also one of the first works to depict homosexuality as natural rather than as a choice.

c. 10 CE

The **WARREN CUP**, an ornate ancient Roman silver drinking vessel, is decorated with two scenes of male couples engaging in sexual acts against a backdrop of rich tapestries and musical instruments. The cup is most likely commissioned by rich members of a Greek community.

c. 220 CE

The Roman Emperor **ELAGABALUS** is considered by modern historians to have been transgender, as he is reported to have favoured women's clothing and to have offered a vast sum of money to the physician who could perform a sex change operation on him.

c. 450 CE

Surviving texts from Liu Song dynasty China depict male homosexuality as a normal facet of life in the late third century, explaining that it is such a regular practice that it affects heterosexual marriages and makes women resentful and jealous.

c. 500 CE

The **MAHABHARATA**, a Sanskrit epic poem from ancient India, contains several LGBTQ+ characters. The most well-known of these is the warrior in the Kurukshetra war named Shikhandi – born Shikhandini – who is assigned female at birth but identifies as male, eventually exchanging gender with a forest spirit and marrying a woman.

c. 750

During the Abbasid Caliphate of the Islamic Empire, Muslim poets such as the Persian-Arab **ABU NUWAS** write lyrical poetry celebrating homosexual love and the charm and beauty of young male lovers.

'Soon the day will come when science will win victory over error, justice a victory over injustice and human love a victory over human hatred and ignorance.'

German-Jewish physician and radical theorist of sexuality and gender Magnus Hirschfeld was one of the most groundbreaking pioneers in the fight for LGBTQ+ rights. Throughout his career, Hirschfeld tirelessly advocated for an acceptance of homosexuality and was the first doctor to research and openly support transgender people, famously supervising Lili Elbe's first sex reassignment surgery in Berlin in 1930. He was revolutionary in his inclusivity, recognising all people across today's understanding of the LGBTQ+ spectrum. In 1897, he established the Scientific-Humanitarian Committee, the world's first gay rights organisation, and in 1919, he opened the Institute for Sexual Science, the world's first sexology institute. After the Nazis' rise to power in 1933, Hirschfeld's institute was burned down, and his studies confiscated. It has taken over a century for the world to catch up with his progressive work.

Magnus Hirschfeld

German

1868–1935

MAGNUS HIRSCHFELD

1

Before Stonewall

1940s to 1960s

LGBTQ+ individuals come together to demand:

- the decriminalisation of homosexuality
- LGBTQ+ rights
- justice after the Stonewall riots

1947

Lesbian
publication and
'America's gayest
magazine' *Vice Versa*
first published

1955

Openly gay singer Billy
Wright releases 'Don't
You Want a Man Like
Me?' performed in drag

1952

Christine
Jorgensen's sexual
reassignment
surgery makes the
front page of *New
York Daily News*

1952

Patricia Highsmith
publishes her tale of
lesbian love *The Price
of Salt* (republished
as *Carol*)

GAY IS GOOD

The 1940s to the 1960s were game-changing decades for the international LGBTQ+ rights movement. Despite the criminalisation of homosexuality in most countries around the world, gay men and women began to organise themselves formally in the wake of World War II, collaborating across national boundaries to protest their rights to social and legal equality.

These first groups defined themselves as 'homophile' organisations, meaning (from the Greek) 'loving the same'. From the Danish Forbundet af 1948 to the French Arcadie and the US Mattachine Society, these organisations provided a forum for the gay community. In 1968, Frank Kameny's slogan 'Gay is Good' was adopted by the North American Conference of Homophile Organisations (NACHO, pronounced 'Nay-Ko') delegates, rejecting the idea that being gay was anything to be ashamed of.

Gradually, this work fighting for equality started to bear fruit: Sweden and Denmark both decriminalised homosexuality in 1944; in 1962 the first US state (Illinois) decriminalised consensual sexual relations between same-sex couples; in 1967, England and Wales followed suit with the Sexual Offences Act; East Germany followed in 1968 and West Germany in 1969.

1956

James Baldwin publishes queer novel *Giovanni's Room*

1959

Some Like It Hot is released, featuring cross-dressing and a same-sex kiss

1967

Craig Rodwell opens the world's first gay book shop, the Oscar Wilde Memorial Bookshop, in New York

1969

Gay avante-garde theatre group The Cockettes is founded in San Francisco

Alongside these legal wins, a new generation of activists, emboldened by the strategies and progress of the civil rights movement, were changing the direction and tactics of the fight for LGBTQ+ rights. Viewing their struggle as part of a larger picture of dismantling broad social structures of oppression, these activists were more defiant in their outlook and demands. At the same time, the LGBTQ+ community in the US began to resist police raids on gay bars, notably Compton's Cafeteria in San Francisco and LA's Black Cat Tavern.

In 1969, the unrest reached breaking point at the Stonewall Inn in New York's Greenwich Village neighbourhood. In an era-defining moment, patrons of the bar and local residents fought back against persecution: a 200-person riot ensued for three nights. The uprising sent a loud message to the world, galvanising an international movement. In its aftermath, a powerful new force emerged: gay liberation.

1940s TO 1960s IN CONTEXT

From throwing off the yoke of empire to the push for gender and racial equality and the fight against dictators, wars and the state, the struggle for queer rights was born among the worldwide liberation movements post-World War II.

1939–1945

WORLD WAR II

World War II (1939–1945) involved and affected almost every country in the world and remains the deadliest conflict in human history with an estimated 70–85 million deaths. This includes an estimated 6 million Jews as well as a still unclear number of homosexuals, thought to be in the thousands, who died during the Holocaust. The USA's development and use of atomic weapons against Japan in 1945 effectively ended the war and led to a nuclear arms race with the Soviet Union in the following decades. With Western Europe recovering from the war, a cold war between the USA and the Soviet Union emerged as the two nations competed to be the world's leading superpower.

1945–1960

POST-WAR DECOLONISATION

A period of decolonisation followed World War II, as nations fought for independence from imperial rule. In India, Gandhi became a global icon for his policy of non-violent protest, which saw India gain its independence from Britain in 1947. In 1960, since dubbed the 'Year of Africa', seventeen countries gained independence from their European colonial rulers. The transition to self-governance was often violent and the legacy of colonial rule is visible in discriminatory anti-gay legislation that, in some cases, exists to this day.

1964

THE CIVIL RIGHTS ACT

The decades-long struggle for equal rights for African Americans won its largest legislative gains during the 1960s. The movement used non-violent strategies such as boycotts, sit-ins and marches to achieve its goals. The Civil Rights Act of 1964 banned discrimination based on race, colour, religion, sex or national origin and ended segregation. That same year, Rev. Martin Luther King Jr won the Nobel Peace Prize for his leadership of the movement.

1968

SOCIAL AND POLITICAL UNREST

The year 1968 was marked by popular rebellion and social unrest, with violent protests against authorities and elites taking place in most European capitals, including Paris, London, Rome, Prague and Berlin, as well as in the US. While there is still much debate on the legacy of the 1968 riots, they are widely regarded as the archetype for the modern protest.

1969

FIRST MAN ON THE MOON

American astronaut Neil Armstrong was the first person to walk on the moon during the Apollo 11 mission in 1969. As part of the Cold War Space Race between the Soviet Union and the USA, the mission was preceded by other great achievements: the first person in space was Russian Yuri Gagarin in 1961, soon followed by the first woman in 1963, Valentina Tereshkova.

1969

THE COUNTERCULTURE MOVEMENT

The Woodstock festival is considered the peak of the anti-establishment counterculture movement that took place in much of the Western world during the 1960s and 1970s. Made up of young people, often born during the post-war baby boom, the counterculture was opposed to the mainstream views of contemporary society, promoting free love, women's rights and a restructuring of traditional economic and family systems.

1960–1979

SECOND-WAVE FEMINISM

Second-wave feminism fought for women's rights within the family, reproductive rights and against legal inequalities. By giving women control over their reproductive health, the increased availability of the contraceptive pill throughout the 1960s was instrumental in giving women the choice to have children, further education and a career. A major victory for the women's movement came in 1973 when the US Supreme Court protected a woman's right to have an abortion in the now famous *Roe vs Wade* trial. However, second-wave feminism has been criticised for failing to include the experiences of lesbian and trans women.

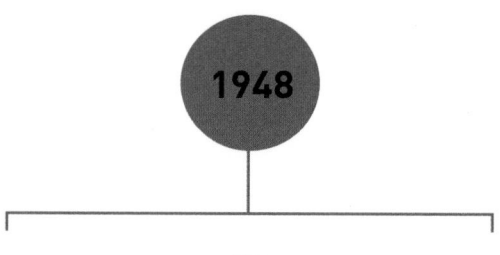

1948

US

BIOLOGIST AND SEXOLOGIST ALFRED KINSEY PUBLISHES THE KINSEY SCALE, REVOLUTIONISING POPULAR THINKING ON SEXUALITY: SEXUAL ATTRACTION HAD PREVIOUSLY BEEN THOUGHT TO BE FIXED AND BINARY. KINSEY PRESENTS ATTRACTION AS FLUID, AND SUBJECT TO CHANGE.

THE WORLD IS NOT TO BE DIVIDED INTO SHEEP AND GOATS. NOT ALL THINGS ARE BLACK NOR ALL THINGS WHITE.

ALFRED KINSEY (1894–1956)
AMERICAN BIOLOGIST, SEXOLOGIST AND
'FATHER OF THE SEXUAL REVOLUTION'

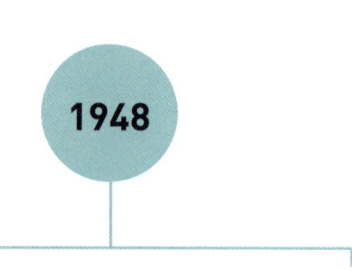

1948

DENMARK

AXEL AXGIL FOUNDS
KRESDEN AF 1948 ('CIRCLE
OF 1948'), ONE OF THE
FIRST LGBTQ+ RIGHTS
ORGANISATIONS IN THE
WORLD. IT IS NOW
KNOWN AS LGBT DENMARK.

1950

FRANCE

ANDRÉ BAUDRY SETS
UP THE FIRST HOMOPHILE
GROUP IN FRENCH HISTORY,
THE ASSOCIATION ARCADIE.
IT WORKS TO SOCIALISE
THE ACCEPTANCE OF
THE GAY COMMUNITY IN
FRENCH SOCIETY, WITH
ITS OWN CLUB HOUSE
AND LITERARY REVIEW.

1950

US

THE MATTACHINE SOCIETY FORMED BY HARRY HAY IS ONE OF THE FIRST GAY RIGHTS GROUPS IN THE UNITED STATES, FOLLOWED FIVE YEARS LATER BY THE FIRST NATIONAL LESBIAN RIGHTS ORGANIZATION, THE DAUGHTERS OF BILITIS (DOB).

1951

THE INTERNATIONAL COMMITTEE FOR SEXUAL EQUALITY (ICSE) IS FOUNDED BY THE PRESIDENT OF DUTCH HOMOPHILE ORGANISATION, THE CENTRE FOR CULTURE AND LEISURE (COC), UNITING EUROPEAN AND US HOMOPHILE ORGANISATIONS IN A TRANSNATIONAL RIGHTS GROUP.

'Be open. Come out. Keep fighting. This is the only way to move anything.'

Born in 1915, Axel Axgil was a true pioneer of the LGBTQ+ movement. A founding member of Kresden af 1948, under his stewardship, the organisation amassed 1,339 members by 1951 and reached a world record of 2,600 by the time he stepped down as chairman in 1952. He campaigned for the right to enter into a civil partnership for decades and was also one half of the first same-sex couple in the world to enter into a registered partnership, having been engaged to his partner for almost forty years. When they finally married in 1989, Axel and his partner, Eigil Eskildsen, merged their first names to create the new surname 'Axgil'.

Axel Axgil
DANISH

1915–2011

AXEL
AXGIL

1957

UK

THE WOLFENDEN REPORT IS PUBLISHED, RECOMMENDING THAT 'HOMOSEXUAL BEHAVIOUR BETWEEN CONSENTING ADULTS IN PRIVATE SHOULD NO LONGER BE A CRIMINAL OFFENCE'. IT LEADS TO THE PASSING OF THE SEXUAL OFFENCES ACT, WHICH LEGALLY DECRIMINALISES HOMOSEXUALITY IN 1967.

1958

EAST GERMANY

PROMINENT PSYCHOLOGIST RUDOLF KLIMMER USES HIS INFLUENCE TO STOP ALL CONVICTIONS FOR SEXUAL ORIENTATION AND SUCCESSFULLY PUSHES FOR LEGALISATION IN 1968.

EQUALITY MEANS MORE THAN PASSING LAWS. THE STRUGGLE IS REALLY WON IN THE HEARTS AND MINDS OF THE COMMUNITY, WHERE IT REALLY COUNTS.

BARBARA GITTINGS 1932-2007
AMERICAN ACTIVIST
FOR LGBTQ+ EQUALITY

DECRIMINALISING HOMOSEXUALITY

Anti-gay stigma has been entrenched in law in many countries around the world. Thanks to the efforts of many brave and tireless campaigners, these laws have gradually been overturned. The chart below shows a selection of the dates of decriminalisation.

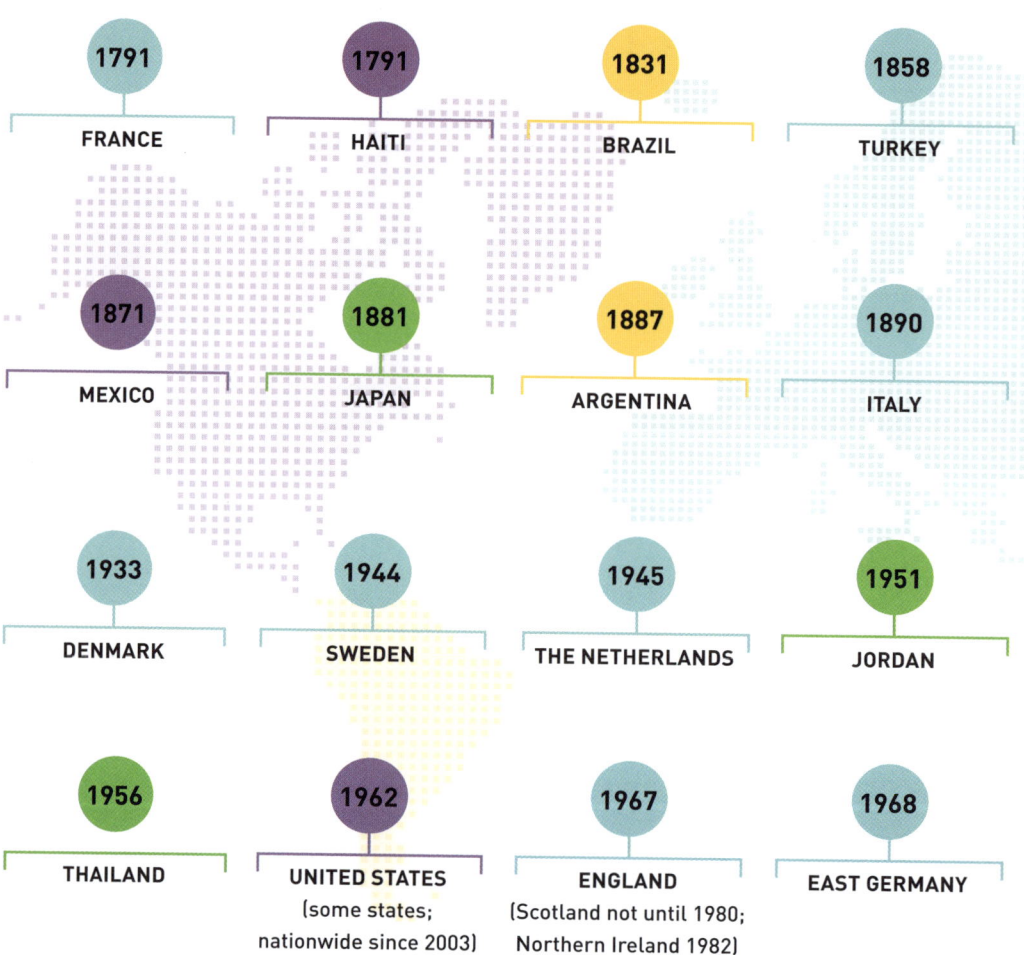

1791 FRANCE	**1791** HAITI	**1831** BRAZIL	**1858** TURKEY
1871 MEXICO	**1881** JAPAN	**1887** ARGENTINA	**1890** ITALY
1933 DENMARK	**1944** SWEDEN	**1945** THE NETHERLANDS	**1951** JORDAN
1956 THAILAND	**1962** UNITED STATES (some states; nationwide since 2003)	**1967** ENGLAND (Scotland not until 1980; Northern Ireland 1982)	**1968** EAST GERMANY

Key Each continent is represented by a different colour throughout the book

- Europe
- Asia
- North America
- South America
- Africa
- Oceania

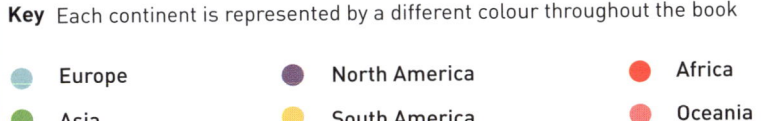

1969
CANADA

1975
AUSTRALIA
(South Australia,
nationwide since 1994)

1979
SPAIN

1986
NEW ZEALAND

1993
RUSSIA

1997
CHINA

1998
SOUTH AFRICA

2000
AZERBAIJAN

2007
NEPAL

2016
BELIZE

2018
INDIA

2019
BOTSWANA

As of 2020, homosexuality remains
illegal in 71 countries around the world

'Women are blessed with two entirely separate systems; one is there for their sexuality ... the other for reproduction. There's no need to get them mixed up.'

Born in London in 1926, Jackie Forster was a broadcaster, reporter and trailblazing lesbian rights activist. After publicly coming out at Speaker's Corner in London in 1969, Forster joined the Campaign for Homosexual Equality (CHE) and dedicated the rest of her life to fighting for LGBTQ+ rights. In 1972 she co-founded the lesbian social group Sappho, which published a monthly magazine until 1981 and held weekly meetings until the late 1980s. She campaigned for the rights of lesbians to become mothers through artificial insemination, and co-wrote *Rocking the Cradle* about lesbian mothers with Gill Hanscombe in 1981. Hanscombe described Forster as being 'that rare individual. She has noble instincts and the noblest of them is to fight for injustice of any kind, not just for lesbians'.

Jackie Forster

ENGLISH

1926–1998

JACKIE
FORSTER

LGBTQ+ ACTIVISM IN PRINT

Magazines played an important role in rallying the LGBTQ+ rights movement and creating solidarity in communities that faced prejudice from the mainstream media.

1896 German writer and anarchist **ADOLF BRAND** publishes the first gay magazine in the world, *Der Eigene* (*The Unique*), an arts and culture magazine that runs for thirty-five years, finally ceasing publication because of the Nazis in the 1930s. Brand is also a member of the first ever LGBTQ+ rights organisation, Magnus Hirschfeld's Scientific-Humanitarian Committee.

1924 Germany is also responsible for the first lesbian magazine in the world, *Die Freundin* (*The Girlfriend*), which is published in Berlin until 1933, when it is forced to shut down by the Nazis. Part-educational, part-political, the magazine mainly publishes short stories and novellas. It aims at creating a community of lesbians, publishing articles about nightspots and cultural events as well as personal adverts.

1952 In the post-war years in Japan, a number of gay groups begin to network. A prominent group is the Adonis club, which for ten years publishes a newsletter featuring cultural essays, erotic material and personal ads. **YUKIO MISHIMA** is one its contributors. It is an essential precursor of 1970s LGBTQ+ magazines in Japan, such as *Barazoku* and *Adon*.

1953 The first gay men's magazine in the US, *One*, is published. Founded in 1952, **ONE, INC.** was born from a discussion of the Mattachine Society. The magazine is sold publicly in Los Angeles and One, Inc. wins a lawsuit against the US Post Office department when it refuses to distribute the magazine on the grounds of obscenity. The One Archives is now one of the oldest LGBTQ+ archive institutions.

1956

San Francisco-based lesbian organisation the **DAUGHTERS OF BILITIS** publishes the first issue of *The Ladder* magazine, which continues until 1972. While it starts as a twelve-page newsletter, its circulation grows quickly. With Barbara Gittings as editor in 1963, it becomes overtly political.

1964

The first gay rights organisation **ASK** emerges in Canada and the Toronto magazine *Gay* is launched. This is the first magazine to use the word 'gay' in its title. It is soon expanded to the US as *Gay International*. But it only lasts two years, shutting down in 1966 due to criminal charges against one of its creators.

1967

The monthly single-page newsletter published by radical gay rights organisation **PRIDE** (Personal Rights in Defence and Education) evolves into a newspaper known as *The Advocate*. It is the longest running LGBTQ+ magazine in the US.

1972

Gay News, Britain's first gay newspaper, is founded in London and later relaunched in magazine format as the *Gay Times*. It is now published both in the UK and the US. The same year sees the launch of the influential British lesbian magazine *Sappho*, founded by 12 women including Jackie Forster, which is circulated until 1981.

1975

The most enduring gay publication in Australia, *Campaign*, is launched just as South Australia finally decriminalises homosexuality. Its name plays on the 'camp' in 'campaign' and its content spans news, political manifestos, event listings, polemic, advertisements, celebrity interviews and photos and gossip.

1979

French magazine *Gai Pied* is founded. The publication is supported by a number of prominent intellectuals who protect the magazine against censorship and often contribute, including Michel Foucault, Serge Gainsbourg, David Hockney and Jean-Paul Sartre. Nevertheless, the minister of the interior threatens to shut the magazine down in 1987; this move is met with protest from many quarters and the minister of culture declares his public support. Circulation ends in 1992.

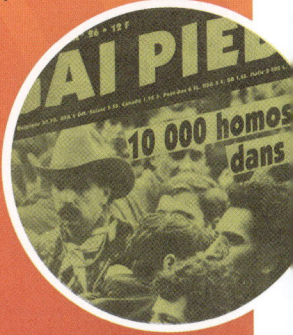

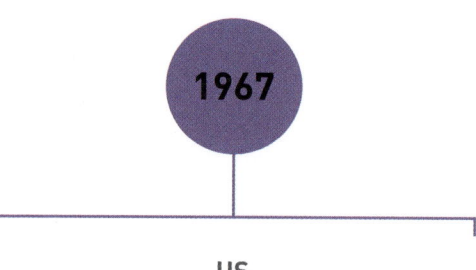

1967

US

PLAIN-CLOTHES POLICE OFFICERS RAID THE BLACK CAT TAVERN IN LOS ANGELES ON NEW YEAR'S DAY. THE RAID PROMPTS A SERIES OF PROTESTS ORGANISED BY PRIDE (PERSONAL RIGHTS IN DEFENSE AND EDUCATION), MARKING THE FIRST TIME 'PRIDE' IS ASSOCIATED WITH THE LGBTQ+ RIGHTS MOVEMENT.

1969

AUSTRALIA

THE ACT HOMOSEXUAL LAW REFORM SOCIETY IS FORMED, A HUMANIST ORGANISATION BASED IN CANBERRA THAT IS CONSIDERED AUSTRALIA'S FIRST GAY RIGHTS ORGANISATION.

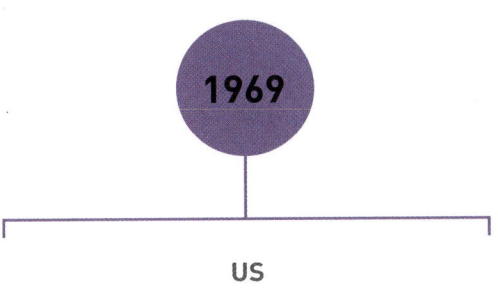

1969

US

POLICE RAID THE STONEWALL
INN, GREENWICH VILLAGE,
AS PART OF A SERIES
OF VIOLENT CRACKDOWNS
ON GAY BARS SERVING
WITHOUT A LICENCE TO
SERVE ALCOHOL. THE QUEER
COMMUNITY FIGHTS BACK,
AND THE UPRISING LASTS
SIX DAYS, TRIGGERING THE
MODERN LGBTQ+ LIBERATION
MOVEMENT IN THE US
AND BEYOND.

1971

FRANCE

INSPIRED BY PROTEST
MOVEMENTS WORLDWIDE,
THE HOMOSEXUAL FRONT
FOR REVOLUTIONARY
ACTION IS FOUNDED, ONE
OF THE FIRST RADICAL GAY
LIBERATION GROUPS
IN FRANCE.

'Darling, I want my gay rights now!'

An outspoken visionary and trailblazing trans, gay liberation and AIDS activist, 'true Drag Mother' and key participant in the Stonewall uprising of 1969, Marsha P. Johnson was one of the architects of the modern LGBTQ+ rights movement. Some credit her with having thrown the first brick in the Stonewall rebellion of 1969, the pivotal protest in which the queer community fought back following a summer of violent and humiliating police raids. In its aftermath, Johnson helped to organise the gay liberation marches in New York that would become Pride; together with Sylvia Rivera, she also established Street Transvestite Action Revolutionaries (STAR) in 1970, an inspirational collective that provided housing and support to homeless queer teens and sex workers in lower Manhattan. When asked, she said the P in her name meant 'Pay It No Mind', a defiant epithet that rejected gender binaries. She continued to organise and fight for LGBTQ+ rights, joining the AIDS advocacy group ACT UP in 1987, until her death in 1992, when her body was found in the Hudson River.

Marsha P. Johnson
AMERICAN

1945–1992

MARSHA P. JOHNSON

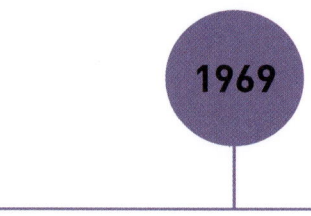

1969

US

IN THE WAKE OF THE STONEWALL RIOTS, THE GAY LIBERATION FRONT (GLF) IS FORMED IN NEW YORK IN 1969: ITS AIM IS TO DISMANTLE SOCIAL INSTITUTIONS SUCH AS GENDER AND THE NUCLEAR FAMILY AND ACHIEVE SEXUAL LIBERATION FOR ALL. IT IS THE FIRST ORGANISATION TO USE THE WORD 'GAY' IN ITS NAME.

WE CAN NO LONGER STAY INVISIBLE. WE SHOULD NOT BE ASHAMED OF WHO WE ARE. WE HAVE TO SHOW THE WORLD THAT WE ARE NUMEROUS.

SYLVIA RIVERA (1951–2002)

AMERICAN GAY LIBERATION AND TRANS
RIGHTS ACTIVIST WHO PLAYED A KEY ROLE
IN THE STONEWALL UPRISING

EQUALISING THE AGE OF CONSENT

To date, 180 countries have brought the age of consent for LGBTQ+ individuals into harmony with the age of consent for heterosexual sex. In some countries, the law is ambiguous, making no distinction between hetero- and homosexual acts.

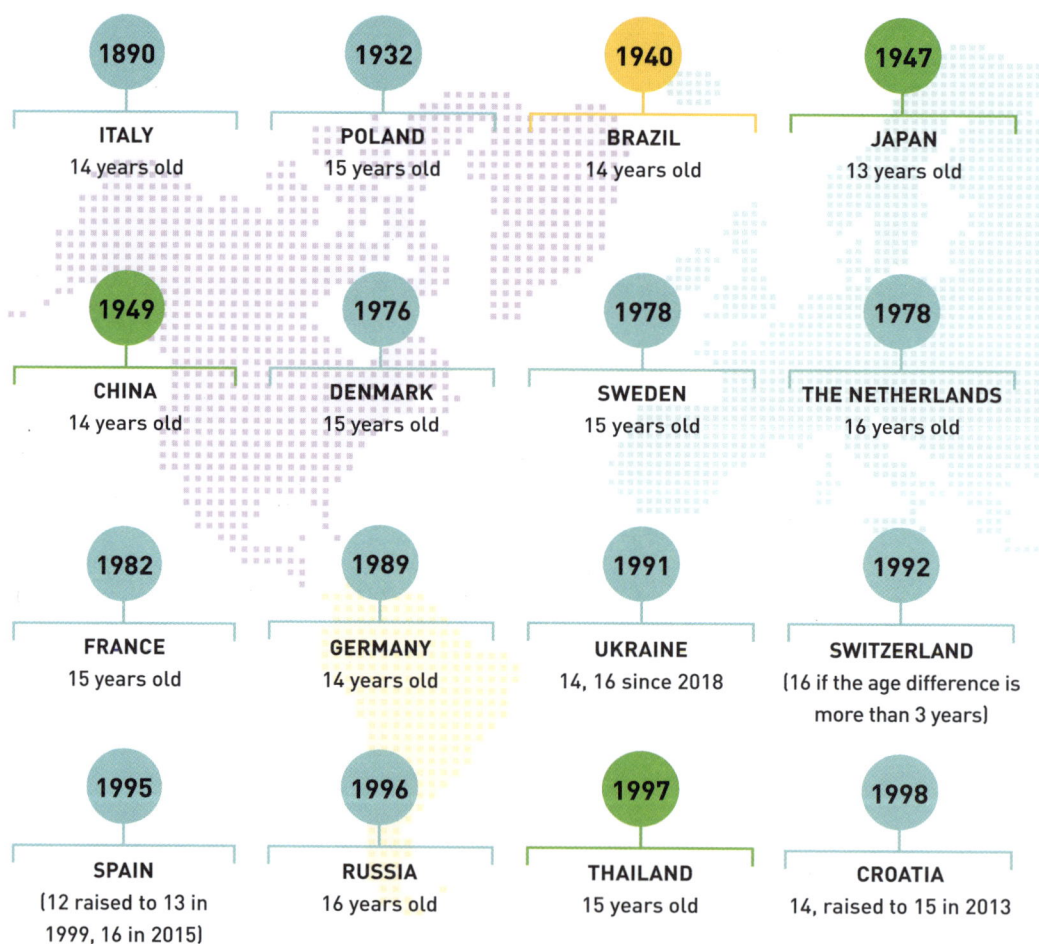

1890

ITALY
14 years old

1932

POLAND
15 years old

1940

BRAZIL
14 years old

1947

JAPAN
13 years old

1949

CHINA
14 years old

1976

DENMARK
15 years old

1978

SWEDEN
15 years old

1978

THE NETHERLANDS
16 years old

1982

FRANCE
15 years old

1989

GERMANY
14 years old

1991

UKRAINE
14, 16 since 2018

1992

SWITZERLAND
(16 if the age difference is more than 3 years)

1995

SPAIN
(12 raised to 13 in 1999, 16 in 2015)

1996

RUSSIA
16 years old

1997

THAILAND
15 years old

1998

CROATIA
14, raised to 15 in 2013

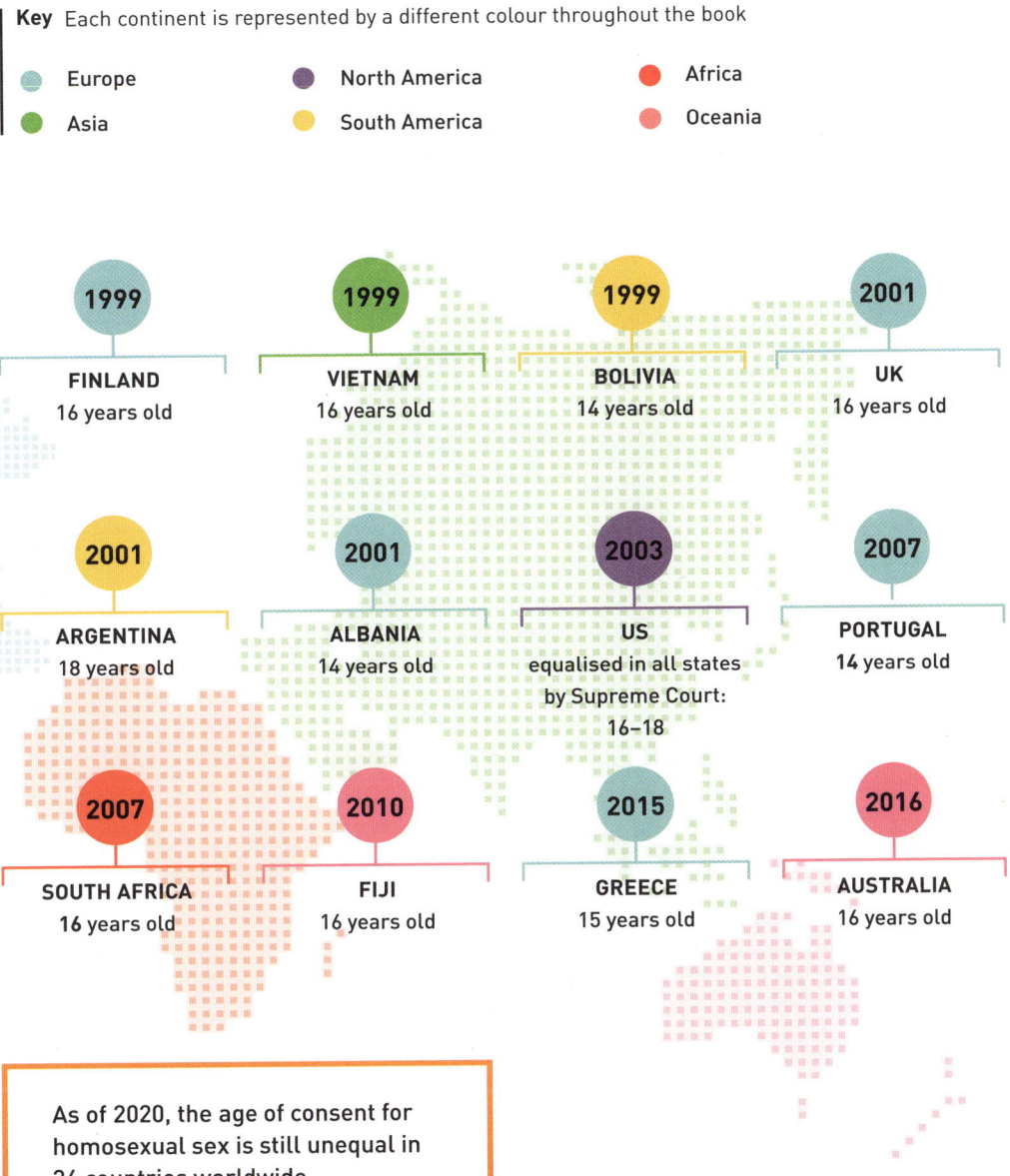

Key Each continent is represented by a different colour throughout the book

- Europe
- Asia
- North America
- South America
- Africa
- Oceania

1999
FINLAND
16 years old

1999
VIETNAM
16 years old

1999
BOLIVIA
14 years old

2001
UK
16 years old

2001
ARGENTINA
18 years old

2001
ALBANIA
14 years old

2003
US
equalised in all states
by Supreme Court:
16–18

2007
PORTUGAL
14 years old

2007
SOUTH AFRICA
16 years old

2010
FIJI
16 years old

2015
GREECE
15 years old

2016
AUSTRALIA
16 years old

As of 2020, the age of consent for homosexual sex is still unequal in 36 countries worldwide.

QUEER ART

Many LGBTQ+ artists have used their work to explore the relationships between gender, sexuality and identity. Challenging society's traditionally held views, they have portrayed the world around them and, in doing so, have actively shaped it.

1930

Part of the Dada movement in Germany during the time of the Weimar Republic, **HANNAH HÖCH** pioneers the photomontage technique, using images from newspapers and magazines to criticise her society's gender roles and encourage women's liberation. Her 1930 work *Marlene* is one of her most controversial photomontages, representing a sexually ambiguous subject. Höch's work is censored by the Nazi regime, which considers it 'degenerate' art.

1945

Established as a foremost post-war painter after his 1945 exhibition of *Three Studies for Figures at the Base of a Crucifixion*, **FRANCIS BACON** is a British artist living openly as a homosexual before it is legalised in the UK in 1967. Throughout his life, he has a series of public affairs that inspire and feature in a number of his works.

1967

DAVID HOCKNEY becomes one of the most popular and influential British artists of the twentieth century. He rises to fame during the 1960s, painting honest depictions of gay love such as *Man in Shower*, *Domestic Scene* and *Peter Getting out of Nick's Pool*, which wins the 1967 John Moores Painting Prize.

1982

KEITH HARING's 1982 *Untitled*, depicting two figures with a heart motif, has been interpreted as a representation of homosexual love and is a perfect example of Haring's vibrant, energetic, graffiti-inspired artworks, dealing with the most complex political issues, and which become symbols of a generation. In 1988, Haring is diagnosed with AIDS and spends the remaining years of his life dedicated to increasing activism and awareness about the disease.

1988 Born in the suburbs of Melbourne, Australia, **LEIGH BOWERY** spends most of his adult life in London, where his flamboyant personal style and taboo-breaking performance art make him an iconic figure of the late 1980s avant-garde scene, first performing in 1988. From 1990 until his death from an AIDS-related illness in 1994, Bowery is a model and muse for Lucian Freud, Freud having seen his performance at the Anthony d'Offay Gallery. Bowery's fearless creativity inspires a generation of artists and performers, from Boy George and Alexander McQueen to Vivienne Westwood and Lady Gaga.

2002 **ZANELE MUHOLI** is a South African artist and visual activist. They rise to prominence in the 2000s for their intimate and powerful portraits depicting black LGBTQ+ individuals, holding their first solo exhibition in Johannesburg in 2002. Muholi sees themselves as a visual activist and art as a tool for social empowerment and visibility. In 2002, Muholi co-founds the Forum for the Empowerment of Women, a black lesbian organisation dedicated to providing a safe space for women to meet and organise events. In 2009 they found Inkanyiso, a non-profit organisation concerned with queer visual activism.

2014 Chinese photographer and poet **REN HANG**'s work reaches a global audience following his first solo exhibition in Copenhagen in 2014. His work is significant for its representation of sexuality in a heavily censored society. He is arrested several times for the erotic undertones in his nude photographs, which show frank depictions of LGBTQ+ love. Hang takes his own life at the age of 29, but his art opens a window on sexual freedom in a conservative society.

2018 **KEHINDE WILEY** uses the visual vocabulary of old European portraits, replacing the subjects with black men. By using a medium that historically invoked glory and prestige, Wiley seeks to challenge existing stereotypes in American society. In 2018, Wiley becomes the first black – and first openly gay – artist to paint an official presidential portrait when Barack Obama chooses him.

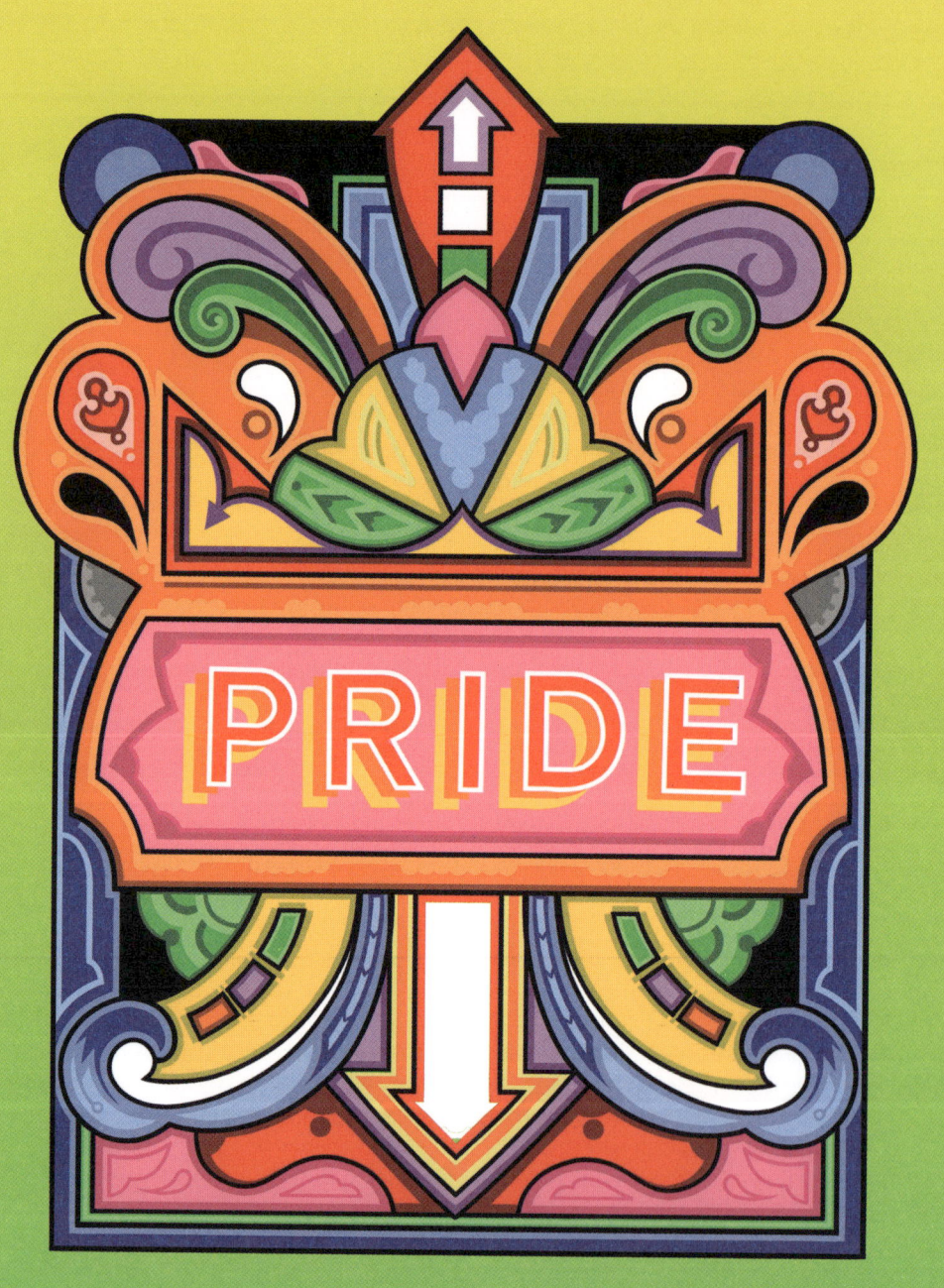

2 LGBTQ+ Liberation

1970s to 1990s

LGBTQ+ communities gain strength and recognition across the globe:

- first pride marches
- LGBTQ+ legislation
- AIDS activism
- achieving political office

1972

That Certain Summer depicts the first gay lovers on TV

1977
On the primetime TV series *Soap*, Billy Crystal plays a gay man

1978

Village People release 'Y.M.C.A.', an instant gay anthem

1982
One of the main characters on *Dynasty* comes out as gay to his family

PRIDE

The last 30 years of the 20th century brought highs and lows for the LGBTQ+ community. Considerable progress was made in terms of rights and freedoms but the arrival of AIDS threatened to reverse many of the gains made in social acceptance.

The Gay Liberation Front (GLF) in both the UK and USA worked collaboratively with feminist and civil rights groups through this period. In New York, Stonewall veterans Sylvia Rivera and Marsha P. Johnson founded Street Transvestite Action Revolutionaries (STAR) in 1970, the first trans youth shelter in North America. In 1972, Sweden became the first country to allow trans people to legally change their sex; Chile followed in 1974. These wins fed a narrative of liberation and hope. By 1980, twenty-two US states had ended all restrictions on sexual relations between consenting adults.

The 1980s brought the devastation of the AIDS pandemic, which affected LGBTQ+ people in huge numbers and threw continuing homophobia into sharp relief. In Europe, the press demonised those who had the 'gay plague', and in the US the Reagan government formally ignored the crisis. In the face of such silence, radical activist groups were formed to put pressure on hastening the development of treatments and services for those diagnosed with HIV/AIDS. The AIDS Coalition to Unleash Power (ACT UP) was established in the US in 1987. Under the banner 'Silence=Death', it prompted the FDA

1993

1994
An Ikea ad shows
an ordinary gay couple
for the first time in
TV advertising

1997

2000
Hilary Swank wins an
Oscar for her portrayal
of trans man Brandon
Teena in *Boys Don't Cry*

Philadelphia is
the first Hollywood
film to deal with
homophobia and AIDS

Ellen
DeGeneres comes
out on the cover of
Time magazine

to speed up approval processes for treatment. In 1987, an estimated 750,000 people took part in the Second National March on Washington for Lesbian and Gay Rights in protest at the government's handling of the AIDS crisis and lack of progress on gay rights. The date of the march, October 11, has been celebrated as National Coming Out Day since 1988.

In the 1990s, LGBTQ+ rights activism continued to affirm that queer rights are human rights, focusing on fighting discrimination and pushing for legal protection and equality. Even as positive changes were enshrined in law, progress was not straightforward, calling for the formation of new action groups to draw attention to continuing homophobia and transphobia, which often took the form of anti-gay violence. One such group, QueerNation, was founded in New York City in 1990. Famous for its confrontational tactics, this grassroots organisation reclaimed the word 'queer'. That same year, Peter Tatchell formed OutRage! Calling for 'protection not persecution', the group protested against the huge rise in gay and bisexual men being arrested for consenting, victimless behaviour.

These organisations drew attention to continuing problems and national governments began to introduce protective legislation, such as the right to asylum for LGBTQ+ people, granted by Canada and the US in 1994. In 1999, Brazil became the first country in the world to ban conversion therapy – treatment based on 'curing' homosexuality'.

1970S TO 1990S IN CONTEXT

As queer culture and lifestyles began to become visible in the mainstream and slowly gain wider acceptance, particularly in the western world, there were still huge strides to be made in the battle to achieve equality.

1973 | GLAM ROCK

Originating in the UK in the early 1970s, glam rock is characterized by performers wearing deliberately outrageous costumes, makeup, and hair. The flamboyant styles were often androgynous and subverted typical gender roles. David Bowie and Elton John were two of the most famous proponents of glam rock, but the genre's influence was widespread.

1975 | THE FALL OF SAIGON

In April 1975, Saigon, the capital of South Vietnam, was captured by the People's Army of Vietnam and the Viet Cong. Referred to as the Liberation of Saigon by the Socialist Republic of Vietnam, the event marked the end of the twenty-year conflict between North and South Vietnam and signalled the beginning of the reunification of the country.

1979 | MARGARET THATCHER

Margaret Thatcher became Britain's first female prime minister in 1979. Throughout the 1980s, she was frequently described as the most powerful woman in the world, her uncompromising politics earning her the nickname the "Iron Lady." She enjoyed a close political relationship with US president Ronald Reagan, based on their shared conservative ideals and belief in free-market economics.

1981 | HIV/AIDS

AIDS was first reported in 1981 with five cases in the US. In 1982, as similar cases appeared – all with impaired immune systems – the disease was named AIDS, 'Acquired Immune Deficiency Syndrome'. Since then, AIDS has killed thirty-five million people worldwide. The LGBTQ+ community was seriously affected by AIDS and misconceptions about the disease's connection to homosexuality resulted in social stigmatisation. Today, the HIV virus that causes AIDS is treatable and people with HIV can live long and healthy lives.

1989 TIANANMEN SQUARE MASSACRE

On 4th June 1989, the Chinese government declared martial law. Troops armed with rifles and tanks fired at demonstrators in what is now known as the Tiananmen Square Massacre, causing thousands of deaths. Among the reasons cited were the weeks of student-led demonstrations that had been held in the Beijing square, in protest against the one-party system and for democracy, freedom of speech and freedom of the press.

1989 THE END OF THE COLD WAR

Following a wave of revolutions overthrowing Soviet rule in Central and Eastern Europe, the Berlin Wall – so long a symbol of political division between East and West – was pulled down. The dissolution of the Soviet Union in 1991 ended the Cold War. New freedoms for LGBTQ+ communities in the former Soviet Union followed. In 1993, under pressure from the Council of Europe, Russia decriminalised homosexuality alongside other former Soviet states: Ukraine in 1991, Estonia and Latvia in 1992, Lithuania in 1993, Belarus in 1994 and Moldova in 1995.

1990s DIGITAL TECHNOLOGY

The World Wide Web, a key tool of the information age, became available to the general public in 1991. The growth of the internet contributed to a period of unprecedented globalisation, allowing faster communication around the world. Through the emergence of social media, LGBTQ+ people have been able to build online communities with people from disparate geographies, diminishing the isolation that had previously been a part of the LGBTQ+ experience.

1994 END OF APARTHEID

In 1990, the F.W. de Klerk government began the process of ending apartheid, releasing Nelson Mandela after twenty-seven years in prison for opposing racial segregation. The first election with universal adult suffrage followed in 1994, and Nelson Mandela became South Africa's first non-white president. In his inaugural speech he declared South Africa would provide equal protection for all its citizens regardless of 'colour, gender, religion, political opinion or sexual orientation'.

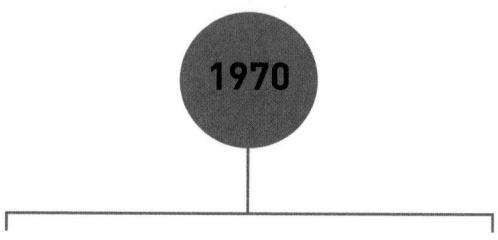

US

ON JUNE 28, PEOPLE RETURN
TO THE STONEWALL INN TO
MARK THE ANNIVERSARY
OF THE RIOTS. THEY
CALL IT 'CHRISTOPHER
STREET LIBERATION DAY',
CELEBRATING WITH A MARCH
IN NEW YORK AND A PARADE
IN LOS ANGELES. THESE
CELEBRATIONS SERVE AS A
CATALYST TO OTHER GAY PRIDE
MARCHES ACROSS THE GLOBE.

WE MUST ROOT OUT THE IDEA THAT HOMOSEXUALITY IS BAD, SICK OR IMMORAL, AND DEVELOP A GAY PRIDE.

**THE 1971 GAY LIBERATION
FRONT MANIFESTO**

'We were sexual liberationists and social revolutionaries, out to turn the world upside down.'

Australia-born Peter Tatchell first came to prominence as a leading member of the London Gay Liberation Front in the early 1970s, organising sit-ins and protests against institutionalised homophobia in the UK. He has since taken this fight for equality across the world, taking part in countless direct-action campaigns in the advocation for queer rights. During the AIDS pandemic he published the first self-help guide for people with HIV and fought for the human rights of those who had been infected. In 2010, a blue plaque was mounted on his London home, celebrating forty years of defending human rights. Tatchell currently spends his time actively supporting human rights and liberation movements worldwide, as he has done throughout his entire life.

Peter Tatchell
BRITISH-AUSTRALIAN

1952–

PETER
TATCHELL

QUEER THEORY

Queer theory is based on the idea that gender is socially constructed and encompasses all sexual acts and identities that are not heteronormative. Feminist and film theorist Teresa de Lauretis coined the term in 1990 at her conference 'Queer Theory: Gay and Lesbian Sexualities' at the University of California, using the expression to redefine the terms we use to define sexuality.

1976

French philosopher and historian of ideas **MICHEL FOUCAULT** publishes the first volume of his *History of Sexuality* in France in 1976. Adopting a constructivist position, he persuasively indicates that the birth of 'homosexuality' dates as a category to the 1870s, arguing that there was no prior corresponding category defining people for those acts. While those acts were indeed condemned (both by religious and civil law), they were not labelled or categorised, in other words those acts were not indicative of a specific 'identity'.

1990

American philosopher and gender theorist **JUDITH BUTLER** is known for challenging traditional conceptions of gender and developing the pivotal theory of gender performativity. She has published extensively; her main works include *Gender Trouble* (1990), *Bodies That Matter* (1993) and *Undoing Gender* (2004). The underlining idea in Butler's work is that all categories we use are essentially socially constructed: gender, rather than being the expression of an 'essence', is performative.

1990

American scholar **EVE KOSOFSKY SEDGWICK**'s work as a queer theorist draws mainly from literature as a space in which to identify queer potential. Some of her most notable works include *Between Men: English Literature and Male Homosocial Desire* (1985) and *Epistemology of the Closet* (1990), in which she discusses the homosexual/heterosexual binary to underline the incoherencies of attempting a definition of homosexuality as an issue of importance for a minority rather then a determining issue for all.

1998

American author, professor and philosopher **JACK HALBERSTAM**, also known as **JUDITH HALBERSTAM**, publishes *Female Masculinity*, in which she theorises the 'bathroom problem', where gender binarism is at its clearest and strictest, offering no place for people who don't fit into those categories. In 2001, she published *The Queer Art of Failure*, in which she argued that failing to live up to heteronormative standards offers room for freedom and creativity.

1999

With the publication of *Disidentifications: Queers of Colour and the Politics of Performance*, Cuban-American academic **JOSÉ ESTEBAN MUÑOZ** highlights the importance of issues of race and ethnicity within queer studies, a perspective often neglected by the field since its emergence in the 1990s. Muñoz went beyond sexuality and introduced the angles of race and identity, focusing on the ways in which queer artists of colour take on, and at the same time, subvert and modify stereotypes. His other seminal work, *Cruising Utopia: The Then and There of Queer Futurity* (2009), sets an optimistic basis for the future of queer communities, which relies on the potential of queer performance art to indicate a utopian futurity.

2000

American professor **ROSEMARY HENNESSY** publishes *Profit and Pleasure*. Taking a materialist approach to sexuality, her queer theory is strictly connected to the structures of late capitalism. She argues that identities that have always been linked to sexuality, such as gender, nationality and race, are in fact a product of capitalism. Hennessey suggests that, while queers have more and more freedom of expression, capitalist society still relies on a traditional binary division of labour.

2004

American literary critic **LEE EDELMAN**'s *No Future: Queer Theory and the Death Drive* studies the state of a society marked by 'reproductive futurism', where the child is the ultimate political referent holding together the present and the future, and where all theory is aimed at a better future. He introduces the figure of the sinthomosexual, disinterested in the future of humanity because of their reproductive incapability, refusing the futurist appeal to the child and embodying the death drive.

PRIDE EVENTS AROUND THE WORLD

The first Pride event was organised by the Gay Liberation Front to commemorate the Stonewall riots. Today, Pride is celebrated in numerous countries around the world, with an annual parade to celebrate LGBTQ+ culture, achievements and legal rights. The map below shows a selection of them and the year in which each held its first Pride parade.

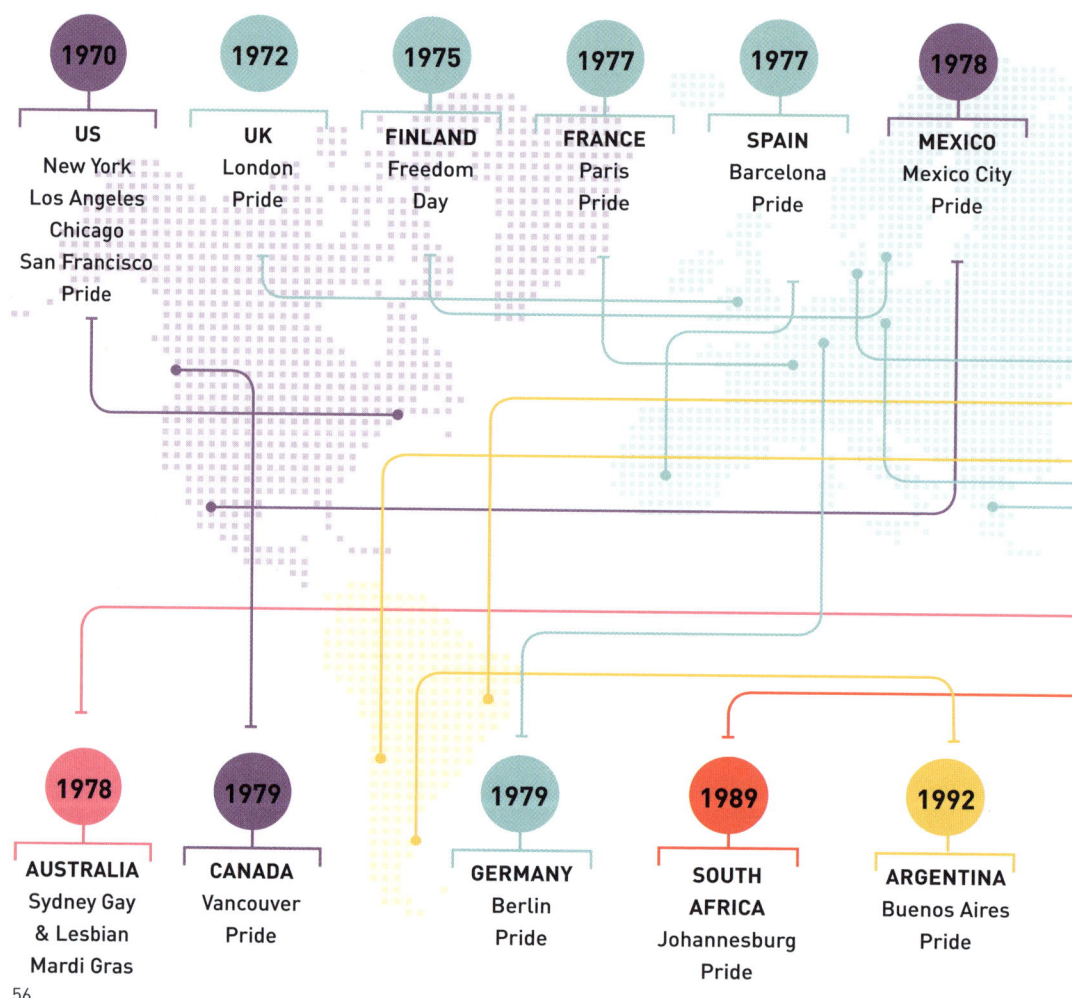

1970

US
New York
Los Angeles
Chicago
San Francisco
Pride

1972

UK
London
Pride

1975

FINLAND
Freedom
Day

1977

FRANCE
Paris
Pride

1977

SPAIN
Barcelona
Pride

1978

MEXICO
Mexico City
Pride

1978

AUSTRALIA
Sydney Gay
& Lesbian
Mardi Gras

1979

CANADA
Vancouver
Pride

1979

GERMANY
Berlin
Pride

1989

**SOUTH
AFRICA**
Johannesburg
Pride

1992

ARGENTINA
Buenos Aires
Pride

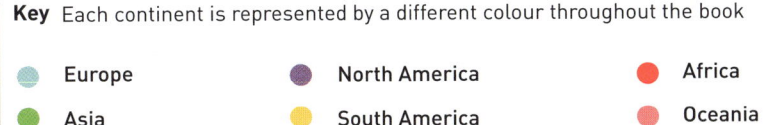

Key Each continent is represented by a different colour throughout the book

- Europe
- Asia
- North America
- South America
- Africa
- Oceania

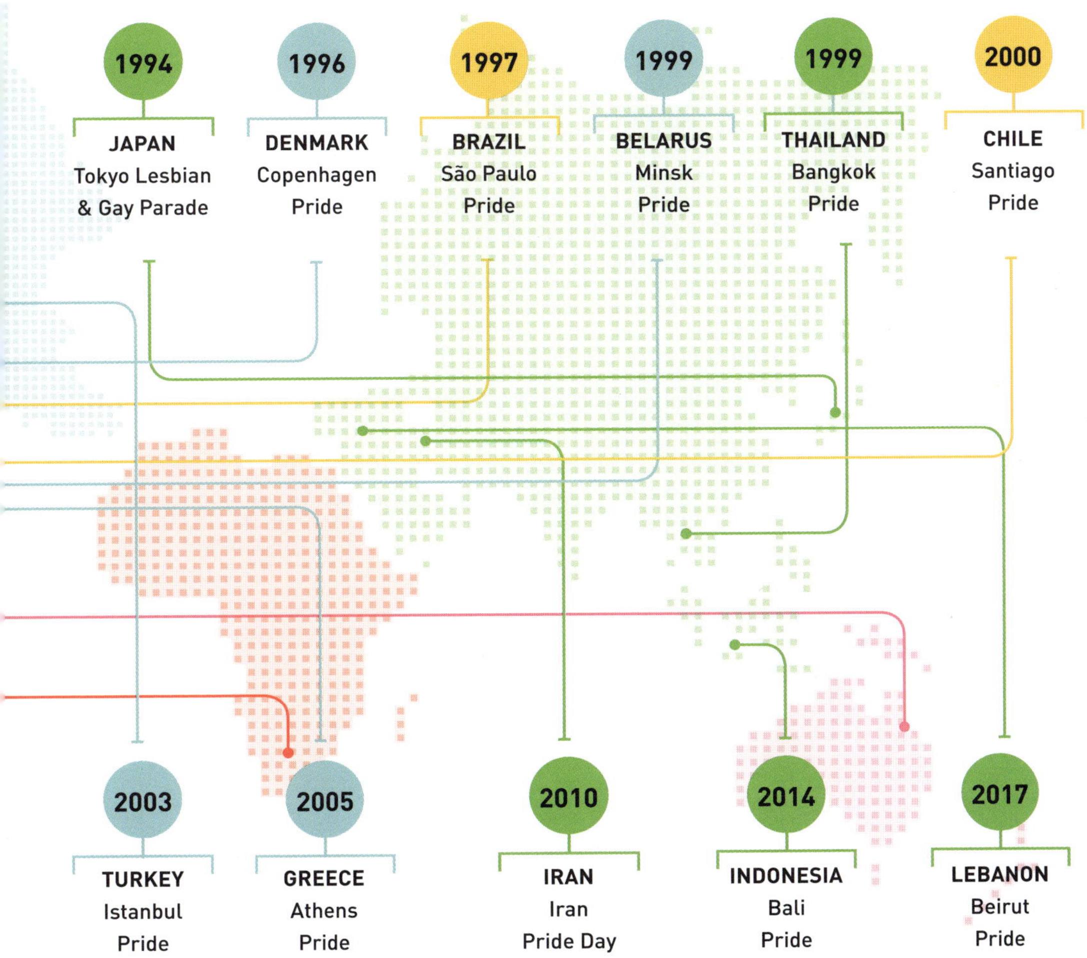

1994

JAPAN
Tokyo Lesbian
& Gay Parade

1996

DENMARK
Copenhagen
Pride

1997

BRAZIL
São Paulo
Pride

1999

BELARUS
Minsk
Pride

1999

THAILAND
Bangkok
Pride

2000

CHILE
Santiago
Pride

2003

TURKEY
Istanbul
Pride

2005

GREECE
Athens
Pride

2010

IRAN
Iran
Pride Day

2014

INDONESIA
Bali
Pride

2017

LEBANON
Beirut
Pride

'Bi, Poly, Switch – I'm not greedy, I know what I want.'

Born in the Bronx, New York, Brenda Howard advocated for LGBTQ+ rights and the inclusion of bisexuality in the early stages of the movement from the time of the Stonewall Inn events until her death. She was the main organiser of the first Pride week in June 1970 and the Christopher Street Liberation Day parade that became its landmark event. She laid the grounds for other parades around the world and became known as the 'Mother of Pride'. A militant activist for all minorities, Howard advocated for causes such as health care, women and people of colour's rights and HIV/AIDS. She was arrested multiple times during her protests. In 1988 she founded the New York Area Bisexual Network and successfully advocated for the inclusion of bisexuality in the 1993 march on Washington.

Brenda Howard
AMERICAN
1946–2005

BRENDA
HOWARD

1972

ITALY

THE FIRST PUBLIC DEMONSTRATION IN DEFENCE OF LGBTQ+ RIGHTS IN ITALY IS ORGANISED BY FUORI, THE FIRST ITALIAN ORGANISATION FOR GAY RIGHTS (FOUNDED THE PREVIOUS YEAR), TO PROTEST AGAINST A CATHOLIC-INSPIRED CONFERENCE ON SEXUAL DEVIANCE.

1972

SWEDEN

SWEDEN DECLASSIFIES TRANSVESTISM AS AN ILLNESS AND BECOMES THE FIRST COUNTRY IN THE WORLD TO ALLOW TRANSGENDER PEOPLE TO LEGALLY CHANGE THEIR SEX.

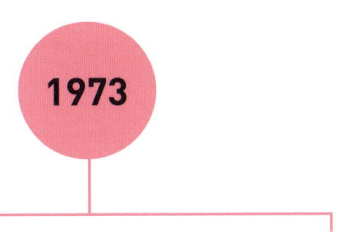

1973

AUSTRALIA AND NEW ZEALAND

THE AUSTRALIAN AND NEW ZEALAND COLLEGE OF PSYCHIATRY FEDERAL COUNCIL BECOMES THE FIRST MEDICAL BODY IN THE WORLD TO DECLARE THAT HOMOSEXUALITY IS NOT AN ILLNESS.

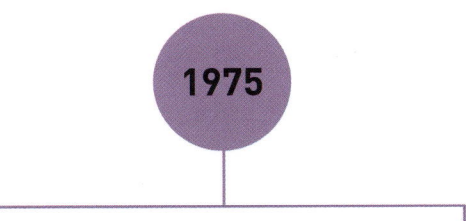

1975

US

21 YEARS AFTER IT WAS FIRST INCLUDED, THE AMERICAN PSYCHIATRIC ASSOCIATION REMOVES HOMOSEXUALITY FROM ITS *DIAGNOSTIC AND STATISTICAL MANUAL OF MENTAL DISORDERS*.

| LGBTQ+ POLITICIANS

The increasing number of LGBTQ+ people elected to political office shows that the political glass ceiling is gradually cracking open. The map below celebrates the political trailblazers.

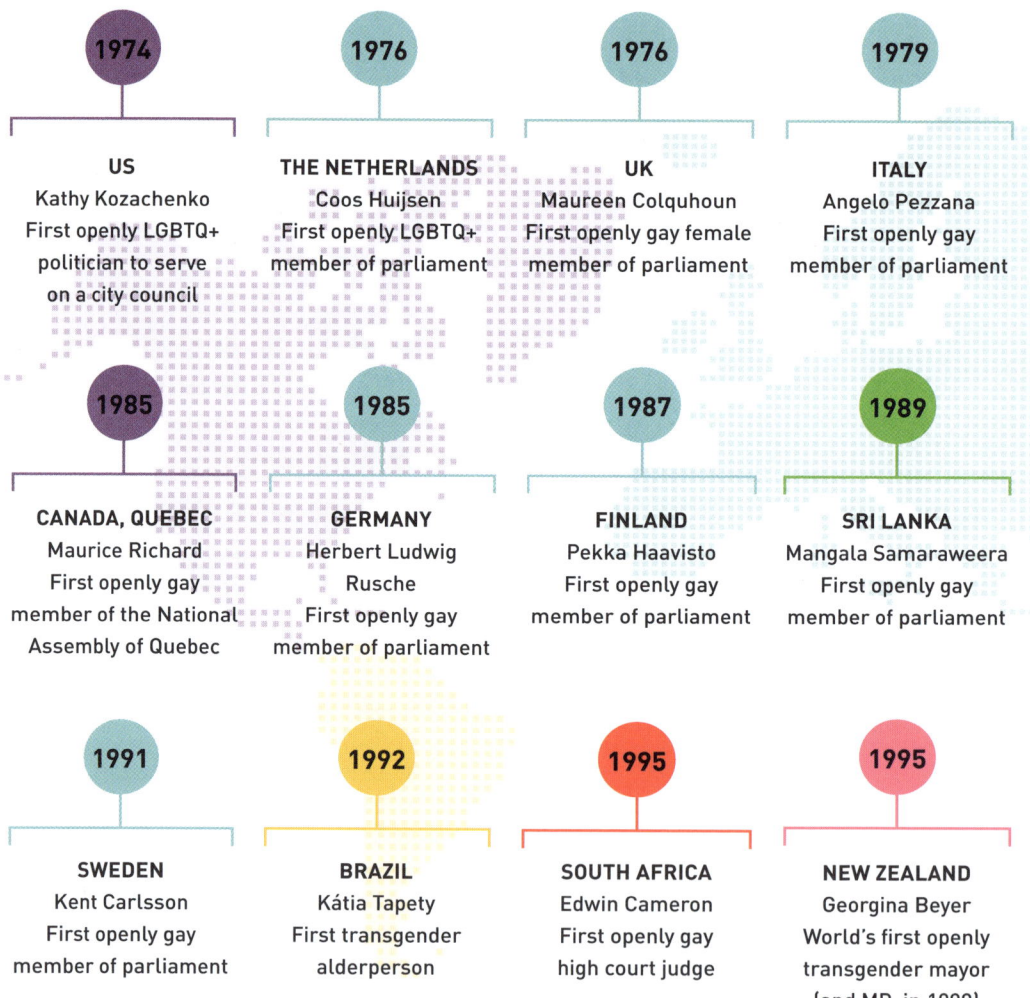

1974

US
Kathy Kozachenko
First openly LGBTQ+
politician to serve
on a city council

1976

THE NETHERLANDS
Coos Huijsen
First openly LGBTQ+
member of parliament

1976

UK
Maureen Colquhoun
First openly gay female
member of parliament

1979

ITALY
Angelo Pezzana
First openly gay
member of parliament

1985

CANADA, QUEBEC
Maurice Richard
First openly gay
member of the National
Assembly of Quebec

1985

GERMANY
Herbert Ludwig
Rusche
First openly gay
member of parliament

1987

FINLAND
Pekka Haavisto
First openly gay
member of parliament

1989

SRI LANKA
Mangala Samaraweera
First openly gay
member of parliament

1991

SWEDEN
Kent Carlsson
First openly gay
member of parliament

1992

BRAZIL
Kátia Tapety
First transgender
alderperson

1995

SOUTH AFRICA
Edwin Cameron
First openly gay
high court judge

1995

NEW ZEALAND
Georgina Beyer
World's first openly
transgender mayor
(and MP, in 1999)

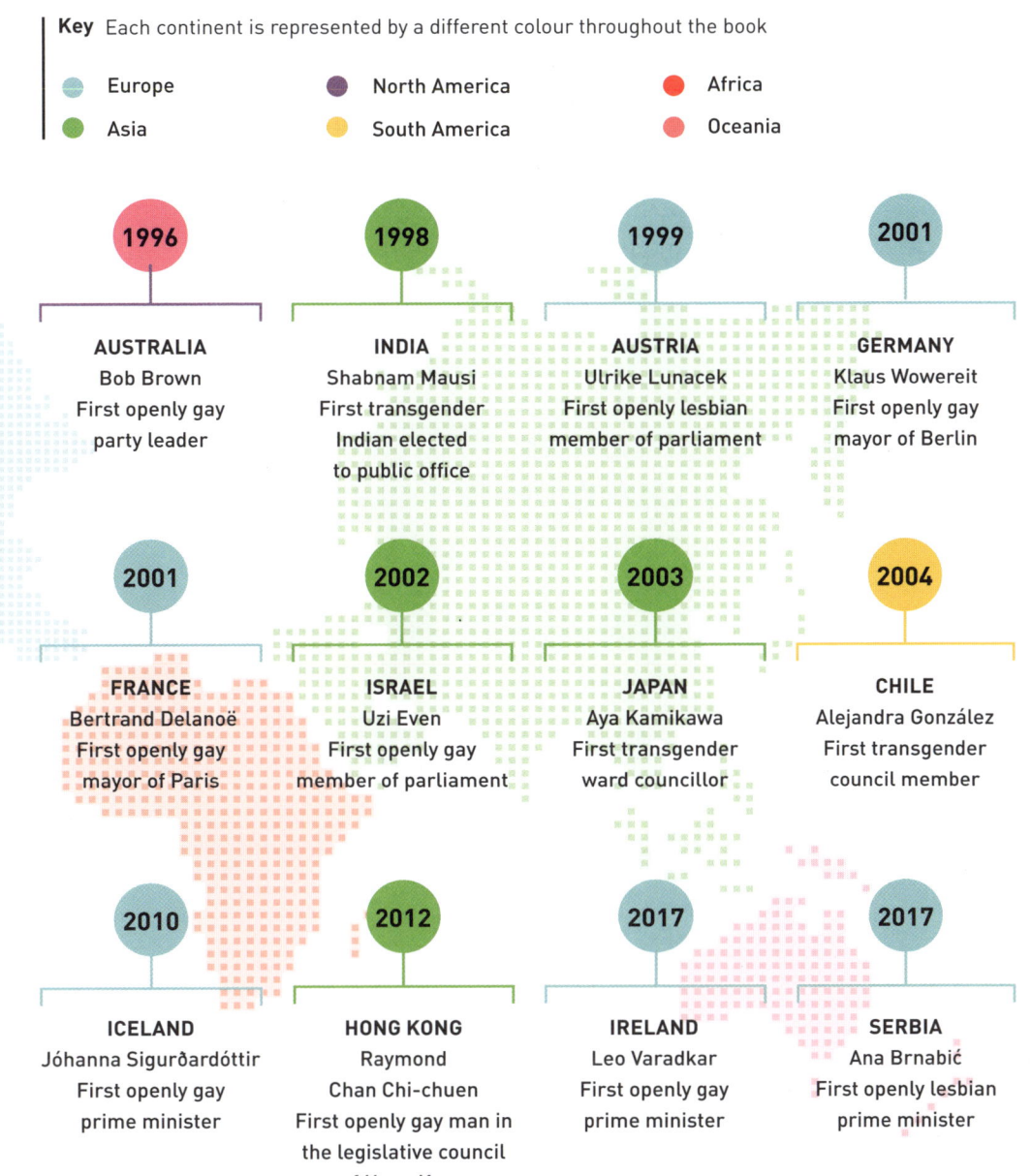

Key Each continent is represented by a different colour throughout the book

● Europe ● North America ● Africa
● Asia ● South America ● Oceania

1996

AUSTRALIA
Bob Brown
First openly gay
party leader

1998

INDIA
Shabnam Mausi
First transgender
Indian elected
to public office

1999

AUSTRIA
Ulrike Lunacek
First openly lesbian
member of parliament

2001

GERMANY
Klaus Wowereit
First openly gay
mayor of Berlin

2001

FRANCE
Bertrand Delanoë
First openly gay
mayor of Paris

2002

ISRAEL
Uzi Even
First openly gay
member of parliament

2003

JAPAN
Aya Kamikawa
First transgender
ward councillor

2004

CHILE
Alejandra González
First transgender
council member

2010

ICELAND
Jóhanna Sigurðardóttir
First openly gay
prime minister

2012

HONG KONG
Raymond
Chan Chi-chuen
First openly gay man in
the legislative council
of Hong Kong

2017

IRELAND
Leo Varadkar
First openly gay
prime minister

2017

SERBIA
Ana Brnabić
First openly lesbian
prime minister

'If a bullet should enter my brain, let that bullet destroy every closet door.'

Harvey Milk was an American gay rights activist and community leader who became California's first openly gay elected official in 1977. During his time as a city supervisor he worked to protect the rights of marginalised communities and sponsored an important law prohibiting discrimination based on sexual orientation. He was assassinated alongside mayor George Moscone on 27th November 1978, after just eleven months in office. For many members of the LGBTQ+ community Harvey Milk was a beacon of hope during a time of widespread discrimination. He was awarded the Presidential Medal of Freedom in 2009 and continues to be celebrated as an LGBTQ+ hero of freedom and equality.

Harvey Milk
AMERICAN

1930–1978

HARVEY
MILK

1987

PRINCESS DIANA OPENS THE FIRST UK WARD DEDICATED TO HIV/AIDS TREATMENT AT LONDON'S MIDDLESEX HOSPITAL. SHE IS PHOTOGRAPHED SHAKING THE HAND OF A MAN DIAGNOSED WITH AIDS IN A TIME WHEN THE ILLNESS WAS BELIEVED TO BE TRANSMITTABLE BY TOUCH.

HIV DOES NOT MAKE PEOPLE DANGEROUS TO KNOW, SO YOU CAN SHAKE THEIR HANDS AND GIVE THEM A HUG. HEAVEN KNOWS THEY NEED IT.

DIANA, PRINCESS OF WALES (1961–1997)

1982

UK

THE DEATH OF TERRY HIGGINS, ONE OF THE EARLIEST DEATHS FROM AIDS IN BRITAIN, LEADS TO THE FOUNDATION OF THE TERRENCE HIGGINS TRUST, THE FIRST CHARITY DEDICATED TO HELPING THOSE SUFFERING FROM THE DISEASE.

1983

WEST GERMANY

A DIVERSE GROUP OF MEDICAL PROFESSIONALS AND GAY MEN FOUND DEUTSCHE AIDS-HILFE (THE NATIONAL GERMAN AIDS ORGANISATION), WHICH DEVELOPS INTO A POWERFUL, INDEPENDENT ASSOCIATION OF AFFILIATE GROUPS ADVOCATING FOR BETTER HIV PREVENTION AND SUPPORT.

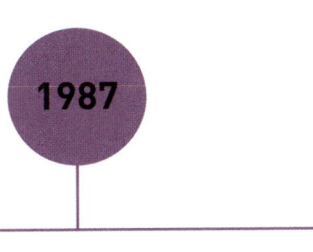

1987

US

LARRY KRAMER FOUNDS
ACT UP (THE AIDS COALITION
TO UNLEASH POWER) IN NEW
YORK CITY. IT PROTESTS THE
SLOW PACE OF THE FEDERAL
DRUG APPROVAL, LEADING TO
NEW REGULATIONS TO SPEED
UP DRUG APPROVAL. THE
MOVEMENT GROWS, SETTING
UP 148 CHAPTERS
IN NINETEEN COUNTRIES.

1994

INDIA

ANJALI GOPALAN FOUNDS
THE NAZ FOUNDATION
IN DELHI. IT LEADS THE
LEGAL BATTLE AGAINST
DISCRIMINATION ON
THE BASIS OF SEXUAL
ORIENTATION AND IS
ONE OF THE FIRST
ORGANISATIONS TO OFFER
CARE AND SUPPORT FOR
INDIVIDUALS IN INDIA
AFFECTED BY HIV/AIDS.

'The dream, the only dream that any ACT UP member carries in his heart is simple: one day AIDS will be eradicated.'

French writer, journalist and LGBTQ+ activist, Didier Lestrade is known for his leading role in the fight against AIDS. He worked for gay publications *Gaie Presse* and *Gai Pied* and founded the main French gay and lesbian magazine, *Têtu*. His fight against AIDS consolidated in 1989 when he co-founded the French Branch of ACT UP, acting as its president for the first three years. In 1992, Lestrade helped found TRT-5, a collective of the main French AIDS foundations, with the aim to protect the rights of people suffering from AIDS. Lestrade has published three books, including a history of ACT UP-Paris and an essay on AIDS.

Didier Lestrade

FRENCH

1958–

DIDIER
LESTRADE

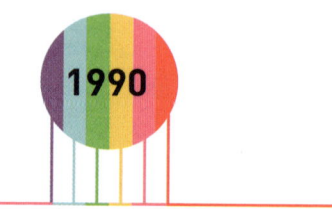

1990

GLOBAL

THE INTERNATIONAL GAY AND LESBIAN HUMAN RIGHTS COMMISSION (IGLHRC) IS FOUNDED IN NEW YORK. IT'S THE FIRST NON-GOVERNMENTAL ORGANISATION DEVOTED TO ADVANCING LGBTQ+ RIGHTS WORLDWIDE. IT IS NOW ACTIVE AS OUTRIGHT ACTION INTERNATIONAL.

1994

CANADA

CANADA GRANTS REFUGEE STATUS TO LGBTQ+ PEOPLE FEARING FOR THEIR WELL-BEING IN THEIR NATIVE COUNTRIES. IN THE SAME YEAR, FEAR OF PERSECUTION DUE TO SEXUAL ORIENTATION BECOMES GROUNDS FOR ASYLUM IN THE US.

1996

UK

P VS. S AND CORNWALL COUNTY COUNCIL FINDS THAT AN EMPLOYEE ABOUT TO UNDERGO GENDER CONFIRMATION SURGERY WAS WRONGFULLY DISMISSED. IT IS THE FIRST PIECE OF CASE LAW IN THE WORLD THAT PREVENTED DISCRIMINATION AGAINST TRANS PEOPLE IN EMPLOYMENT OR VOCATIONAL EDUCATION.

1998

ECUADOR

ECUADOR BECOMES THE FIRST COUNTRY IN THE AMERICAS (AND THE THIRD COUNTRY WORLDWIDE) TO PROTECT SEXUAL ORIENTATION IN ITS CONSTITUTION. DISCRIMINATION IS PROHIBITED IN ALL AREAS, FROM EMPLOYMENT TO THE PROVISION OF GOODS AND SERVICES.

'Your silence will not protect you.'

American writer, feminist and civil rights activist, Audre Lorde was born in New York City by Caribbean immigrants. She affirmed her identity as a lesbian and a poet while studying in Mexico, and she played a pivotal role in the gay cultural scene of Greenwich Village when she returned to New York. Lorde worked many years as a librarian before starting to teach, and being a black lesbian woman in the predominantly white and male environment of academia affected her life, work and social activism in the 1970s and 1980s. Lorde contributed greatly to feminist theories and race studies and her poetry is an empowering and free expression of her identity as – in her own words – 'black, lesbian, mother, warrior, poet'.

Audre Lorde
AMERICAN

1934–1992

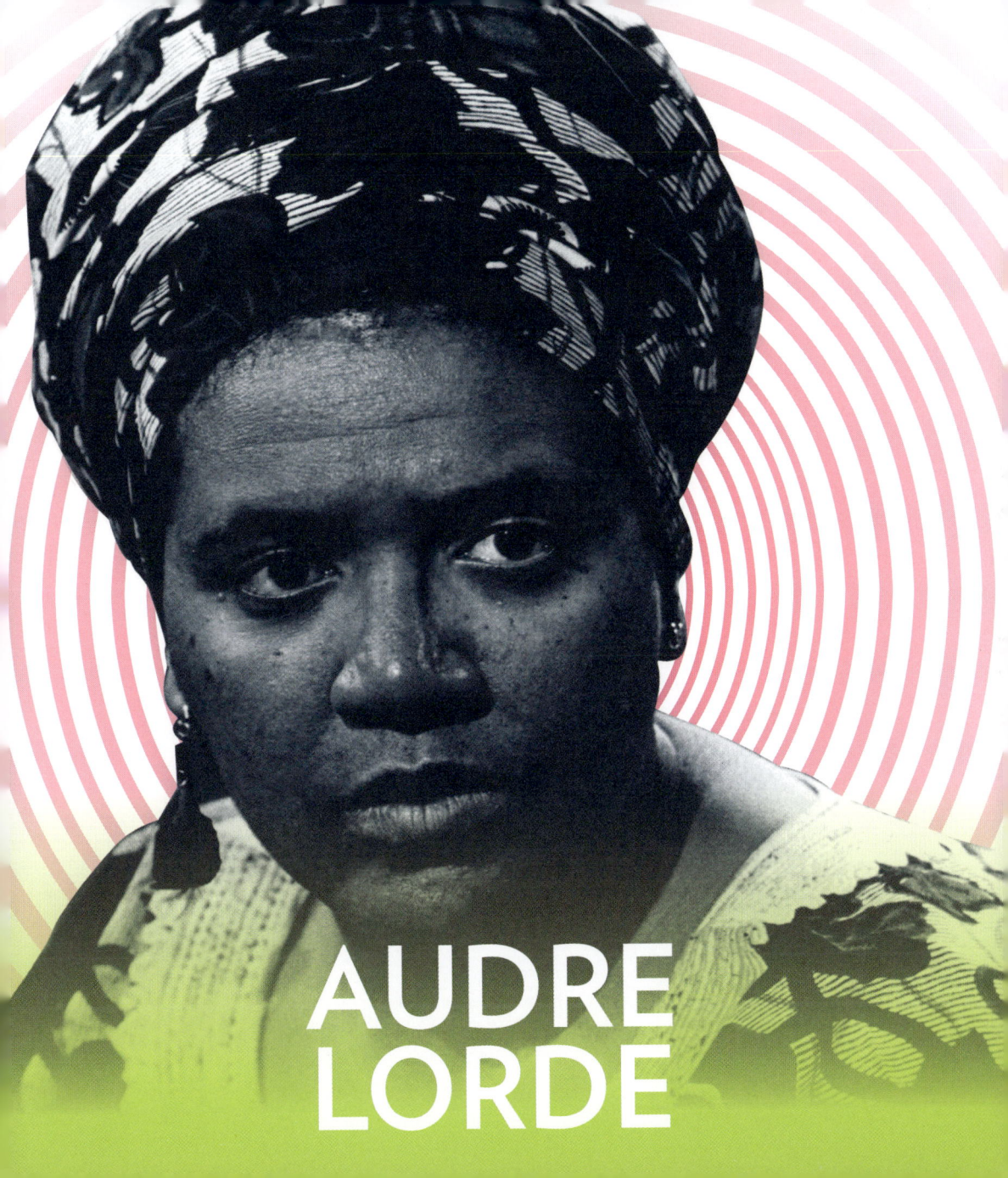

AUDRE
LORDE

QUEER LITERATURE

LGBTQ+ stories provide wonderful insights into the experience of being lesbian, gay, bi and trans. Not only have these works enabled the LGBTQ+ community to rally around a core of meaningful texts, they have also helped non-LGBTQ+ people to gain a better understanding of their fellow humans.

1949 Japanese author **YUKIO MISHIMA** publishes *Confessions of a Mask* in which a young man comes to terms with his sexual identity in rigid imperial Japan and is forced to hide his true feelings for his male classmate behind a mask.

1956 American Beat poet **ALLEN GINSBERG** publishes his radical poem 'Howl', revolutionising queer identity. Its violent resplendent verse gives voice to long-stifled LGBTQ+ communities in the late 1950s. It remains fresh, shocking and entertaining.

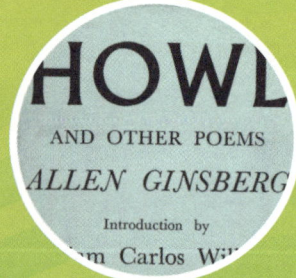

1956 **JAMES BALDWIN**, an African-American novelist, playwright and activist, publishes what is now agreed by many to have been the greatest novel of his career – *Giovanni's Room*. In it, American protagonist David, living alone in Paris, meets Giovanni, an Italian bartender, prompting a profound exploration of homosexuality, bisexuality and what it means to be a man.

1982 African-American author **ALICE WALKER** publishes *The Color Purple*, a novel that tackles race, gender and sexuality within a family against the backdrop of 1930s Georgia. Although the book sparks controversy and is immediately targeted by censors, it garners critical acclaim, and Walker becomes the first black woman to win the Pulitzer Prize for Fiction.

1985

English writer **JEANETTE WINTERSON** publishes her first novel, *Oranges Are Not the Only Fruit*, a semi-autobiographical story in which Jeanette, adopted by an English Pentecostal family and raised to be a missionary, realises that she is attracted to another girl and has to leave her home and church behind.

2010

Puerto-Rican writer **LUIS NEGRÓN** publishes his debut short story collection, *Mundo Cruel*, which chronicles the lives of a queer community in the Santurce neighbourhood of San Juan in Puerto Rico. The book has been reprinted five times in Spanish, and its English translation won the Lamda Literary Award for Gay Fiction in 2014.

2012

The first openly gay Moroccan writer and filmmaker **ADBELLAH TAÏA** publishes *Infidels*, a semi-autobiographical novel that gains him recognition on a global scale. Violent and powerful, the book tells the brief life story of Jallal, the son of a prostitute, who grows up to become a jihadi.

2015

Nigerian-American novelist and short-story writer **CHINELO OKPARANTA** publishes her debut novel, *Under the Udala Tree*, which documents the passionate relationship between two young refugee girls displaced by the Nigerian Civil War.

3 21st-Century Rights

2000 until today

LGBTQ+ rights enter
the mainstream agenda:

- same-sex marriage
- transgender rights
- family rights and adoption
- formal apologies to
  the LGBTQ+ community

2000

2000
*Buffy the Vampire
Slayer* shows TV's
first committed
lesbian relationship

2005

2009
Modern Family debuts
on ABC, depicting
a gay couple and their
adopted daughter

*Dawson's
Creek* shows the
first gay kiss on
US primetime TV

*Brokeback
Mountain* is released,
going on to win three
Academy Awards

WE'RE HERE, WE'RE QUEER

The march towards LGBTQ+ equality picked up pace during the early twenty-first century as the movement gained increased visibility and media attention. Same-sex marriage became a reality for millions of LGBTQ+ couples around the world and trans rights were put firmly on the political map.

The Netherlands led the way for other countries to follow when they legalised same-sex marriage in 2001. As of 2020, same-sex marriage is legal in thirty countries, mainly in Europe and the Americas. A ruling by the European Court of Justice in 2018 granted same-sex spouses of EU citizens the same residency rights as heterosexual spouses under the bloc's freedom-of-movement laws.

In 2012, trans rights activists in Argentina secured a landmark victory as the country passed the Gender Identity Law, granting individuals the right to define their own gender identity on official documents, without first having to receive counselling or surgery. Another cause for celebration came in 2018, when the World Health Organisation (WHO) removed transgenderism from its list of mental health disorders.

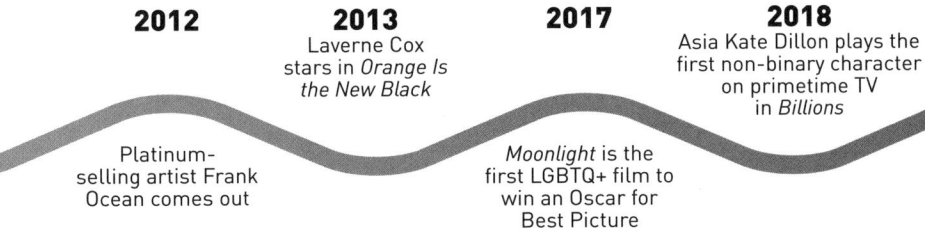

2012
Platinum-
selling artist Frank
Ocean comes out

2013
Laverne Cox
stars in *Orange Is
the New Black*

2017
Moonlight is the
first LGBTQ+ film to
win an Oscar for
Best Picture

2018
Asia Kate Dillon plays the
first non-binary character
on primetime TV
in *Billions*

Progress for trans rights met with backlash in some areas, indicating the persistence of prejudice and hostile opinion. Victories for trans athletes attracted criticism from the general public and other athletes. When Canadian trans woman cyclist Rachel McKinnon broke records, winning a track world championship title in 2018, she received more than 100,000 hate messages on social media. Despite this, trans rights continued to gain prominence and the increasingly online world gave the trans community better visibility as well as facilitating communication and education via online activism.

The 2000s saw considerable progress in the fight for equal rights in the military. By the end of its second decade, the number of countries that allowed gays and lesbians to serve openly had risen to more than fifty from just a handful twenty years earlier. Inclusion of trans people, however, has been slower, with US President Donald Trump reinstating the ban on transgender troops in 2017. Despite this setback, the number of countries that allow transgender troops to serve openly is growing and many are taking steps to ensure their armed forces are free from discrimination against LGBTQ+ individuals.

| 21ST CENTURY IN CONTEXT

The rise of the internet allowed liberation movements, including the fight for LGBTQ+ rights, to become truly global, with people across the world galvanized by communication platforms and empowered unprecedented access to education online.

2001

9/11 AND THE WAR ON TERROR

After the 11th September terrorist attacks on the World Trade Center and the Pentagon by Islamic terrorist group al-Qaeda, the United States government launched a 'war on terror', an international military campaign aimed at radical terrorist networks. The campaign and its name have been widely criticised and President Barack Obama formally ended it in 2013.

2007/8

GREAT RECESSION

In the years following the financial crisis of 2007/8 many parts of the world experienced a period of sustained economic decline. The IMF labelled the Great Recession the most severe economic meltdown since the 1930s and it caused political instability in many of the affected countries.

2009

BARACK OBAMA

When Barack Obama became the USA's first black president in 2009, it was seen as evidence of the progress made since the civil rights movement of the 1960s. In his election campaign, Obama pledged to expand state health care and end US military involvement in Iraq and Afghanistan. He was awarded the Nobel Peace Prize in 2009, and during his presidency, the US government made significant progress for LGBTQ+ rights.

2010s

ARAB SPRING

The Arab Spring saw a series of protests and rebellions taking place in North Africa and the Middle East in the early 2010s, in response to oppressive regimes and low standards of living. In a region where LGBTQ+ people still suffer from discriminatory laws and persecution, many activists hoped the revolutions would usher in a new era of equality but, with the exception of Tunisia, the Arab Spring gave way to a period of instability, counter-revolution and civil war that came to be known as the Arab Winter.

2013 | POPE FRANCIS

Elected in 2013, Pope Francis became the first pope from the Americas, and the first non-European pope for over 1,000 years. In the same year he was named gay magazine *The Advocate*'s Person of the Year for his assertion that the Catholic Church must welcome all people, regardless of sexuality. In 2016 he spoke in favour of transgender people receiving pastoral care, but his views on gender identity have been criticised. While there is still a way to go, Pope Francis has made progress for an institution that has, historically, seen homosexuality as a sin.

2016 | THE RISE OF RIGHT-WING POPULISM

In Europe and the US, the politics of the mid-2010s was dominated by the rise of the right wing. Still recovering from the Great Recession of the late 2000s, far-right politicians throughout Europe tapped into fears of mass-immigration amid the European Refugee Crisis. The 2016 Brexit vote and election of Donald Trump to the US presidency are considered part of this trend towards de-globalisation and nativist stances. In Brazil and the Philippines, far-right leaders Jair Bolsonaro and Rodrigo Duterte have been criticised internationally for their discriminatory comments against LGBTQ+ people.

2017 | THE #ME TOO MOVEMENT

Tarana Burke's hashtag #metoo is popularised by American actress Alyssa Milano, encouraging women around the world to share their experiences of sexual violence. The campaign gained huge momentum, being used by more than 4.7 million on Facebook in the first twenty-four hours, and spreading to more than eighty-five countries with sister hashtags such as #YoTambien in Spain, #BalanceTonPorc in France ('expose your pig') and #quellavoltache in Italy ('that time when').

2018 | CLIMATE EMERGENCY

Climate change became a topic of international concern during the 2010s, as the effects of human-caused global warming began to be seen. Rising temperatures and an increase of natural disasters caused governments, populations and scientists to take action. Swedish student Greta Thunberg's school strikes and powerful speeches made her a global symbol of the protest movement.

2004

FRANCE

THE MAYOR OF BÈGLES, IN FRANCE, CELEBRATES A HOMOSEXUAL MARRIAGE AS AN ACT OF DEFIANCE. WHILE BOTH HE AND THE COUPLE ARE SUED AND THE MARRIAGE ANNULLED, THEY SUCCEED IN RAISING THE QUESTION OF GAY MARRIAGE IN THE COUNTRY.

THE DENIAL OF
GAY MARRIAGE SENDS
A PREJUDICE MESSAGE.
OUR YOUTH DESERVE A
FAIR AND HOPEFUL FUTURE
WITH GOVERNMENT THAT
VALUES US EQUALLY.

LADY GAGA (1986–)
AMERICAN SINGER, ACTRESS
AND LGBTQ+ ADVOCATE

'Love is so simple and spiritual. It is not related to social status, age or even sexual identity.'

Sociologist Li Yinhe played a large role in increasing public acceptance of LGBTQ+ groups in mainland China during her time at the Chinese Academy of Social Sciences. In 1992, she and her husband published the first major study into underground Chinese LGBTQ+ subcultures entitled *Their World: A Study of Homosexuality in China*. She also used her position to submit several proposals to the Chinese National Congress calling for the legalisation of same-sex marriage. Since retiring from academic life in 2012, she continues to contribute to public discourse on sexual minorities through her blog, revealing that she had been in a long-term relationship with a transgender man since her husband's death.

Li Yinhe
CHINESE

1952–

LI
YINHE

SAME-SEX MARRIAGE

As of 2020, gay marriage is legal in thirty countries in the world. A further 13 countries, mostly in Europe, allow civil unions and registered partnerships for same-sex couples, but not marriage. Three countries recognize same-sex marriages entered into elsewhere.

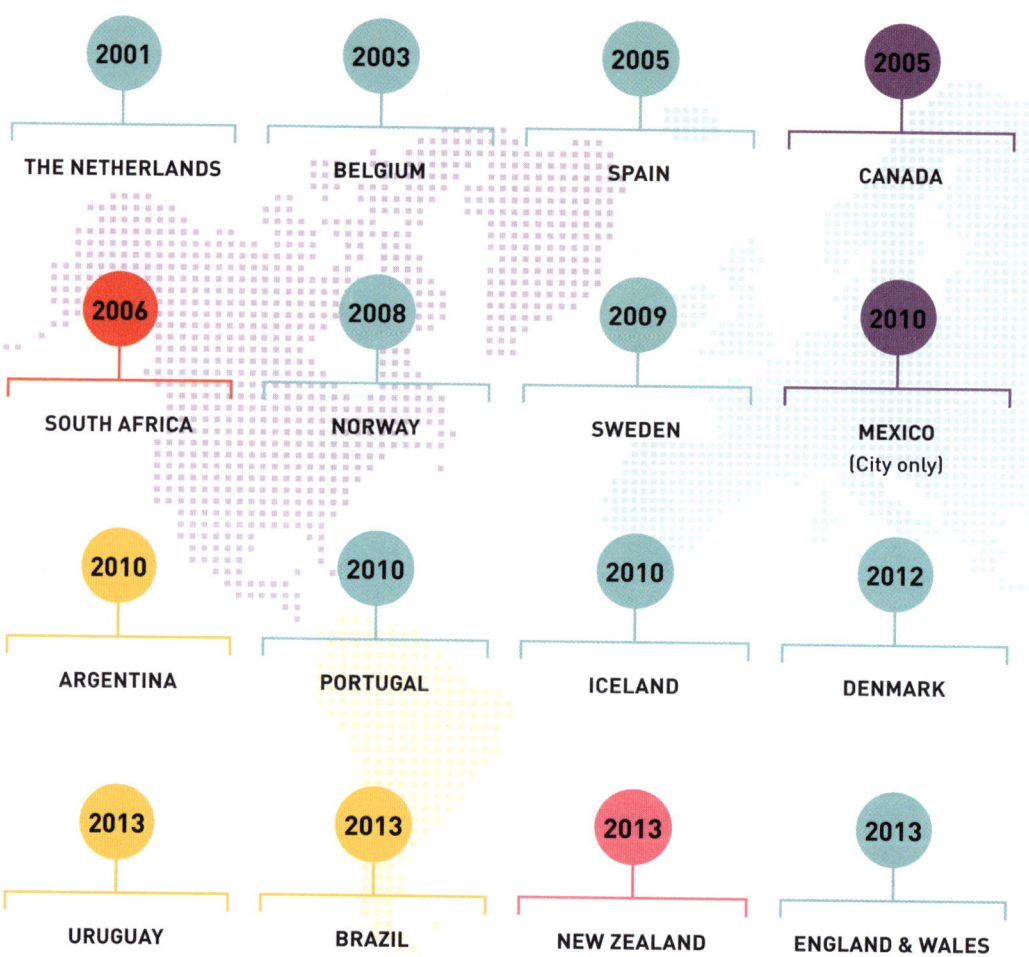

2001	2003	2005	2005
THE NETHERLANDS	BELGIUM	SPAIN	CANADA

2006	2008	2009	2010
SOUTH AFRICA	NORWAY	SWEDEN	MEXICO (City only)

2010	2010	2010	2012
ARGENTINA	PORTUGAL	ICELAND	DENMARK

2013	2013	2013	2013
URUGUAY	BRAZIL	NEW ZEALAND	ENGLAND & WALES

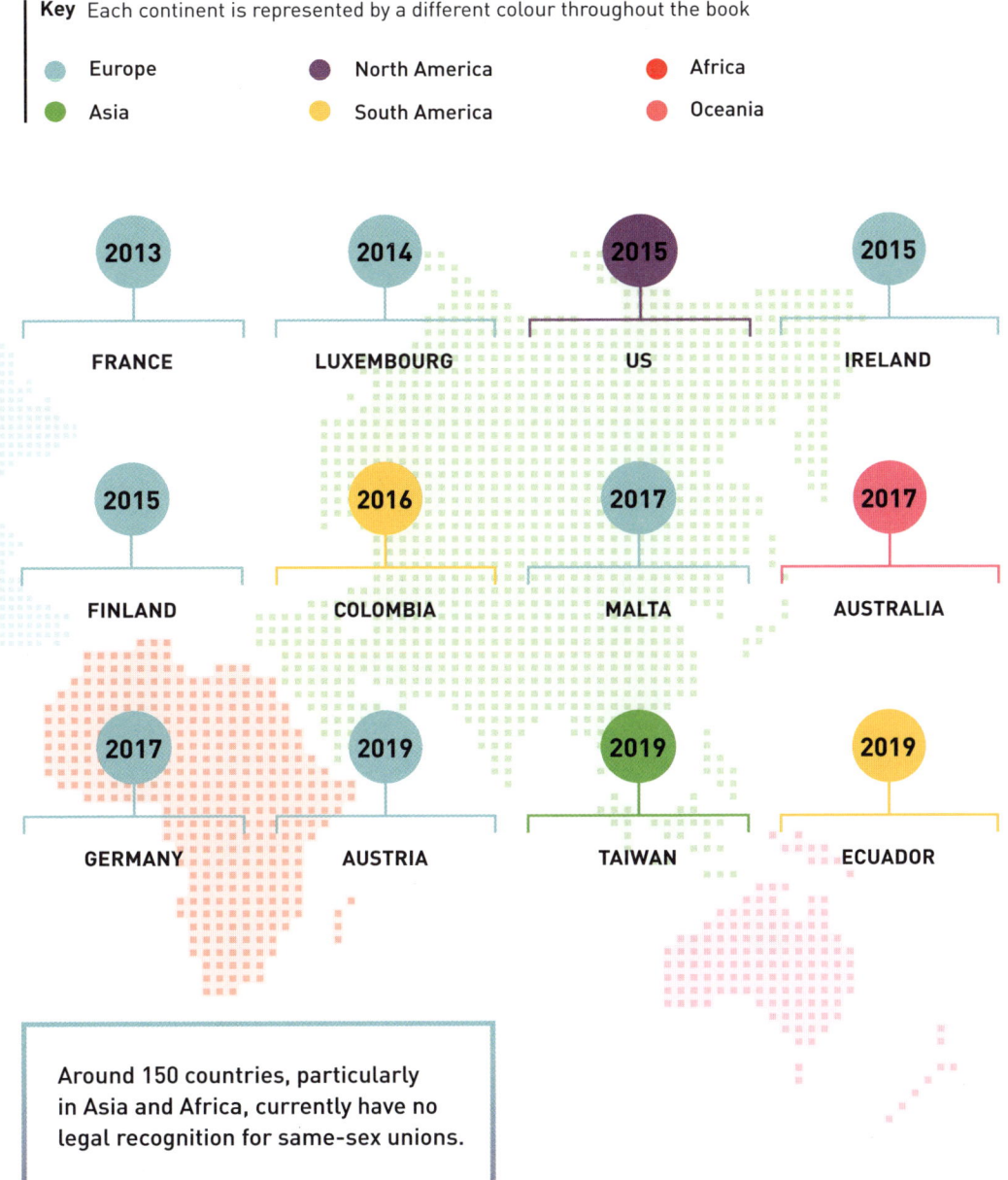

Key Each continent is represented by a different colour throughout the book

- Europe
- Asia
- North America
- South America
- Africa
- Oceania

2013
FRANCE

2014
LUXEMBOURG

2015
US

2015
IRELAND

2015
FINLAND

2016
COLOMBIA

2017
MALTA

2017
AUSTRALIA

2017
GERMANY

2019
AUSTRIA

2019
TAIWAN

2019
ECUADOR

Around 150 countries, particularly in Asia and Africa, currently have no legal recognition for same-sex unions.

2002

2001

SOUTH AFRICA

SUSANNE DU TOIT SUCCESSFULLY FIGHTS FOR HER PARTNER ANNA-MARIE DE VOS TO HAVE LEGAL PARENTAL RIGHTS OVER HER ADOPTIVE CHILDREN, LEADING SOUTH AFRICA TO BECOME THE FIRST AFRICAN COUNTRY TO ALLOW ADOPTION BY SAME-SEX COUPLES.

THE NETHERLANDS

THE FIRST COUNTRY IN THE WORLD TO LEGALISE SAME-SEX MARRIAGE BECOMES THE FIRST COUNTRY TO GRANT ADOPTION RIGHTS TO SAME-SEX COUPLES.

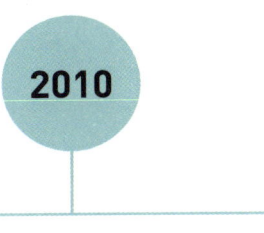

2010

FRANCE

LAWYER AND ACTIVIST CAROLINE MÉCARY WINS A TEST CASE FOR GAY PARENTS WHO HAVE CHILDREN OVERSEAS, REPRESENTING A FRENCH-AMERICAN LESBIAN COUPLE, WHERE THE FRENCH PARTNER ADOPTS THEIR CHILD CONCEIVED THROUGH ARTIFICIAL INSEMINATION IN THE US, BUT IS NOT RECOGNISED AS THE LEGAL PARENT UNDER FRENCH LAW.

2017

US

AFTER A SUPREME COURT RULING ON 26 JUNE, ADOPTION BY LGBTQ+ INDIVIDUALS OR SAME-SEX COUPLES BECOMES LEGAL IN ALL FIFTY STATES.

LGBTQ+ COUPLES

Artists, writers and activists in history have defended the right to choose who to love through their work and in their private lives. Here are some iconic LGBTQ+ couples that proudly lived their relationships in the public eye.

1907 | American author **GERTRUDE STEIN** meets **ALICE B. TOKLAS** in Paris; their relationship starts immediately and lasts until Stein's death thirty-nine years later. The couple host a salon in their home in Paris, which becomes a meeting place for American expats and members of the Parisian avant-garde.

1922 | **VIRGINIA WOOLF** and **VITA SACKVILLE-WEST** meet for the first time, at a time when Sackville-West, ten years younger, is the more accomplished and successful writer of the two. While both women are married, their romantic relationship is facilitated by the open-minded environment of the Bloomsbury Group and supported by both husbands. Their relationship lasts ten years, eventually evolving into a long-lasting friendship.

1947 | American playwright **TENNESSEE WILLIAMS** meets and falls in love with Italian-American actor **FRANK MERLO**. The actor becomes Williams' personal secretary and the two have a long-term relationship for fourteen years. Shortly after their separation, Merlo is diagnosed with a severe form of lung cancer and Williams cares for him until his death in 1963.

1958 | French fashion designer **YVES SAINT LAURENT** meets industrialist and patron **PIERRE BERGÉ**. They begin a relationship and together launch Yves Saint Laurent Couture House in 1961, for which Bergé acts as CEO until it closes in 2002. Their romantic relationship lasts until 1976, but they remain lifelong friends and, according to *The New York Times*, were joined in a civil union (French PACS) a few days before Saint Laurent's death in 2008.